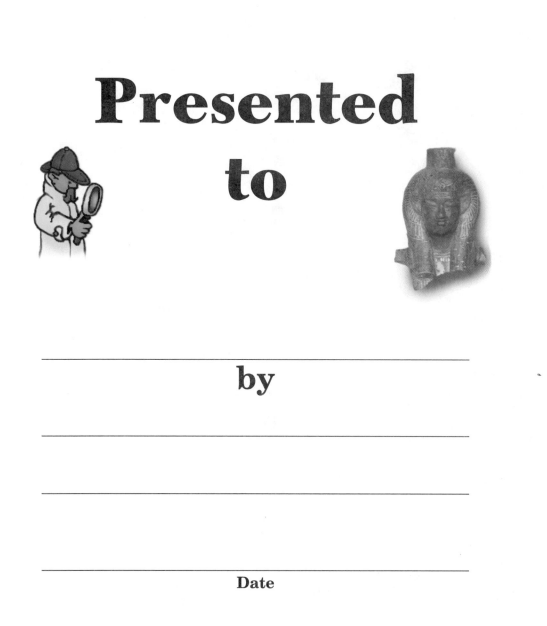

Presented to

by

Date

THE
AMAZING
EXPEDITION
BIBLE

The Amazing Expedition Bible
Text © 1997 by Mary Hollingsworth, Shady Oaks Studio, Bedford, Texas.
Illustrations © by Christopher Gray
Research assistants: Charlotte Greeson, B.A., M.M.Ed.; Lydell Humphries, B.A., M.Ed.

Mind Meld memory scriptures quoted from the *International Children's Bible, New Century Version*, copyright © 1986, 1988 by Word Publishing, Dallas, TX 75234. Used by Permission.

Produced by Educational Publishing Concepts, P. O. Box 665, Wheaton, Illinois 60189.

Published by New Kids Media™, in association with Baker Book House Company, P. O. Box 6287, Grand Rapids, Michigan 49516–6287.

ISBN: 0-8010-4328-X

Printed in the United States of America

THE AMAZING EXPEDITION BIBLE

Linking God's Word to the World

Mary Hollingsworth

*Illustrated by
Christopher Gray &
Daniel J. Hochstatter*

NEW
KIDS
MEDIA

Published and
distributed in
association with

BAKER
A DIVISION OF
Baker Book House Co

Contents

THE OLD TESTAMENT

95093

LISTS

Preface

All aboard! You have just bought a ticket for the adventure of a lifetime with *The Amazing Expedition Bible*. This exciting book will take you on a fascinating journey with God's people from their creation until today and beyond.

Oh, the People You Will Meet!

As the story of God's people and their world unfolds, you'll meet kings and queens, musicians and poets, martyrs and madmen. You'll encounter angels and demons, giants and witches, fast friends and mortal enemies. You'll meet heroes and villains, babies and older people, thieves and priests. Get ready to contact the most incredible people who have ever lived since the world began.

Oh, the Places You Will Go!

This great expedition will take you to interesting and exciting places, such as palaces, prisons, temples, terrors, cities, and countries. You'll climb the Great Sphinx, explore the catacombs, scale Mt. Sinai, and walk through the Red Sea on dry ground. You'll stroll through the streets of Jerusalem with Jesus, go to war with Antony and Cleopatra, be lost at sea with the apostle Paul, and ride along the Great Wall of China. It's truly the journey of a lifetime!

Oh, the Things You Will See!

As you turn the pages of *The Amazing Expedition Bible*, you'll witness the invention of marvelous tools and machines, see miracles and death-defying feats, watch great battles, encounter flaming bushes that don't burn up, attend the first Olympic Games, and watch gladiators fight to the death in the Roman Coliseum. You'll also see the first ship sail around the south tip of Africa, ride in the Trojan Horse as it enters the city of Troy, and march into the Promised Land with Joshua and God's people.

The Right-Order Bible

For the very first time, you will be able to read the entire story of God's people in the right historical order. The Bible is not organized as a story. It's organized by subject—all the books of God's law are together, all the books of history are together, and like that. Because the Bible stories are not always in the right historical order, it's hard to remember which Bible story came first and which one came next. *The Amazing Expedition Bible* will help you by putting all the major

Bible stories in the right order by the dates they probably happened. It will be one long, complete story of how God has loved and cared for his special people throughout history. It's like reading a novel, rather than the Bible in its usual arrangement.

The Word in the World

Also, because we study world history in regular school and Bible history in Sunday school, it's hard to know which world events happened at the same time as certain Bible events were taking place. Once again, *The Amazing Expedition Bible* will help by linking world history events and Bible events together by date to give you a more complete picture of the world in which God's people lived.

For instance, did you know that Shadrach, Meshach, and Abednego may have read Æsop's Fables when they were growing up just as you do? Here's something interesting, too: the Egyptians of Moses' day may have eaten pancakes for breakfast just as you do... but they didn't have any syrup! And did you know that Noah and his family could have eaten popcorn on the ark while they watched it rain?

Historical Dates

To help you get a good idea of which events happened when, you will find dates beside the many Bible and world events in this book. However, these dates are often just estimated. In many cases no one knows for sure when certain things happened, not even our best scholars and historians, especially in the earliest part of history. We have tried to use the dates that respected historians and scholars have assigned to these events, but sometimes even the scholars don't agree. So, we ask you to understand that these dates are only approximate and not absolutely accurate.

How to Read Historical Dates. Historical dates either come before Christ lived (B.C.) or after he was born (A.D.). All dates are counted from zero, either backward for dates before Christ (B.C.) or forward for dates after his birth (A.D.). Starting at the year zero, then, you would say that fifty years before Christ was 50 B.C. And fifty years after his birth was A.D. 50. The farther away from the birth of Christ you get, the higher the number of the year. For instance, Noah may have lived about 3000 years before Christ came, or 3000 B.C. Today we live about 2000 years after Christ's birth; so, our new century will be called A.D. 2000.

History Mysteries

The Amazing Expedition Bible will challenge you with some ancient unsolved mysteries, too, both from world history and from the Bible. You'll have to use your best detective talents to try and solve these "History Mysteries." For instance, where was the Garden of Eden located? Was there really a lost continent called Atlantis? Is Jonah the only person who was ever swallowed by a giant fish and lived to tell about it? And can you explain the weird legend of the Minotaur Monster? These intriguing mysteries will bring you many hours of fun and learning.

MindMeld

Another feature you'll like about this Bible is called "MindMeld," which gives you a verse from the Bible to help you remember that story or lesson. It means that you will be melding (joining) your mind with the mind of God.

Get on Board!

So, off we go on this amazing expedition into the world of God's Word. I pray that you will find the adventure to be as fun, exciting, and interesting as I did. May God bless you on your journey.

Mary Hollingsworth

Here is what you'll find in The Amazing Expedition Bible

The Amazing Expedition Bible is an extraordinary new tool that shows how the Bible stories fit into the order of history. This Bible is your guide to Bible times, and contains a wealth of information about what the world was like at different times throughout Bible history. Each page includes fascinating facts, details, pictures, and maps that will expand your understanding of what it was like to live in the time of the Bible. As you look at particular stories you may be familiar with, you'll be introduced to other information that you've heard about at school, or that may be entirely new to you. Most important though is understanding how all of this fits together!

Timeline- This handy tool shows you the approximate year that a particular Bible story took place. Below the timeline, other events that took place in history that may not be mentioned in the Bible are shown.

Sidebars- Throughout this Bible, you'll find interesting articles that explain some aspect of the world in which the Bible story took place. Each of these articles were written to help you see more about the culture, geography, politics, or other issues.

It's a fact- You will find this feature scattered throughout the Bible helping you learn some amazing detail about life in Bible times or a Bible truth to live by.

Did You Know That. . . The Bible is full of curious things that have enthused students ever since it was written. This feature will help you join thousands of people down through the years who have answers to their questions about the Bible.

Bible Mystery- Everyone loves a good mystery! We have picked out many of the mysteries of the Bible and solved them just for you.

Introductory material- Each section in this Bible begins with a section that

shows how the last story leads to the next story. Sometimes many years
have passed between stories, and you need to know what has happened since.

Bible Story- There are sixty different Bible stories which will give you the story of
God's people from Genesis to Revelation. The stories are based on actual Bible
stories, but have had the difficult words removed so you can understand
them better. In some places, we have added some details from world history which the
Bible doesn't include.

Special sections- There are seven sections that are about important subjects:
Literature & Theater, Religion/Philosophy & Learning, Visual Arts, Science/
Technology & Growth, Daily Life, History & Politics, and Music.

Illustrations- Every single page in this Bible includes colorful pictures that
show things as they were or their remains. These pictures will give you
valuable clues to discover the history of Bible times.

History Mysteries- Ever wonder how the Egyptians built the pyramids? Why
did they build the pyramids? These brief Mysteries will unlock for you some
of the secrets of the ancient world.

Maps- Sometimes it is hard to know where an event in the Bible took place
compared to the present world. Our maps will help you see exactly where
to locate these important places.

Mind Meld- People who have loved God's Word have memorized it for
thousands of years. These sections are to help you "hide God's Word in your
heart and mold your mind to match His."

Lists- There are lists to help you find exactly what you are looking for: Bible
stories in alphabetical order, historical articles in alphabetical order by title,
and a list of important events in historical order.

Acknowledgments

No book is produced by one person, especially a book like this one. Publishing is a huge team effort. And so, my heartfelt gratitude goes out to...

God, without whose blessings nothing worthwhile is ever accomplished. To him alone be glory and honor.

My scholarly predecessors. Not being a scholar myself, I have relied on their mountain of wisdom and historical work to compile this volume for a younger-than-usual audience. I am both humbled by your amazing skills and thankful for your dedication in preserving the world of God's people.

Charlotte Greeson, my forever friend, for locating valuable resources, research assistance, educational advice, patience, and constant encouragement.

Lydell Humphries, my long-time friend, for a Herculean task of researching, organizing, and writing companion materials for both this book and the accompanying CD-ROM.

Jerry Watkins, Todd Watkins, Jim Elwell, and the whole team at Educational Publishing Concepts, for not only catching the vision of this book, but also for expanding and enriching the vision. You're the best!

Richard Baker and Baker Book House for making the dream a reality for children everywhere.

"God loved the world so much

that he gave his only Son...

so that whoever

believes in him may not be lost,

but have eternal life.

God did not send his Son into the

world to judge the world guilty,

but to save the world

through him."

John 3:16-17

The Old Testament

God Creates the World	Noah and the Flood	The Tower of Babel
CREATION	3000–2500 B.C.	2400 B.C.

Bronze implements are in common use in the Middle East.	3000 B.C.—The city of Troy is first inhabited.	2800 B.C.—Building of Stonehenge began.	2400 B.C.—Egyptians begin to use papyrus as a writing material.

In the Beginning...

Genesis 1–3

History & Politics

The first great civilization known in the world was the country and people of Sumer. Their influence as a nation was probably at its height during this time.

Literature & Theater

The first written language was most likely created by priests in the country of Sumer. They drew pictures on clay tablets with a sharp reed.

God! Nothing else existed. The earth was empty. No plants, no animals, no fish, and no people could be found. Land and seas all ran together. Everything was totally dark because no sun, moon, or stars hung in the inky-black void. Houses, streets, and cities had never been built. Computers, airplanes, and cars had not even been imagined yet. Only the great Spirit of God—the wonderful Spirit of love—was alive when time began.

Have you ever wondered where we all came from, and how we got here? Who are we, and where are we going anyway? What are we supposed to do with this time called "life"? What happens after we die? Or can we live forever? Who is God, and how did it all begin?

People have been trying to answer these questions for as long as they have been on earth. And today, we must answer them for ourselves. Here is the story of how it all happened, as told by God himself, because he's the only one who really knows.

The Story of Creation

In the beginning God created the sky and the earth. And during the next six days, he created everything else in the world and around the world—earth and skies, land and seas, animals, birds, fish, and plants. He made the sun, moon, and stars. And finally, he made people.

God loved the people he had made most of all. He loved them so much that he wanted them to be like him. He named the first two people Adam and Eve, and he put them in charge of everything else he had made. Then he gave them a beautiful garden for a home. And every night God came and walked in the pretty garden in the cool evening breeze and talked to the people he loved.

HISTORY MYSTERY

Where is the Garden of Eden? And does it still exist today? For clues, read Genesis 2:8–14 in your Bible.
Answer: No one knows for sure, except God himself who planted it.

Religion, Philosophy & Learning

The concept of "zero" in math was probably understood for the first time during this period of time.

Visual Arts

White, painted pottery was probably being made in both Egypt and southeast Europe at this time.

Music

People have always loved music. Harps and flutes were being played in Egypt in these early days.

21

Although its origin is not known, fire had been discovered and was in use. And rice was being grown in China. Do you think they had fried rice?

Daily Life

Birthday celebrations were being held. And children at birthday parties might have been given pony rides because horses were being tamed at this time.

A Snake in the Grass

One day an evil snake came into the garden. It showed Eve some delicious fruit that grew on the tree in the center of the garden, and it talked her into eating some of the fruit. But God had told Adam and Eve not to eat fruit from that tree. Eve ate some of it anyway; then she gave some to Adam, and he ate it, too.

God was very sad when the people he loved so much did not obey him. Because he was honest and just, he had to punish Adam and Eve for doing wrong. So he put them out of the garden forever. And they had to work hard to raise their

It's a FACT!

No one really knows exactly when Creation happened. But the first year recorded on the Jewish calendar is 3760 B.C. That's over 5,750 years ago!

food and make their own clothes. He also punished the snake by making it crawl on its belly in the dirt forever. (That's why snakes don't have legs today! They have to slither instead of run.)

"In the beginning God created the sky and the earth."

Genesis 1:1

Does God Really Exist?

Some people don't believe that God really lives and acts in our world today. Here are five proofs that God does exist. Perhaps you can share these with your friends who aren't sure about God.

1. *Movement.* We know that the world is in motion. It turns on its axis, and it orbits around the sun. But nothing moves unless it is forced to move by something else. So who or what put the world into motion before any other force existed? God.
2. *Nothing happens by itself.* For example, a table doesn't just appear out of nowhere. It must be made by a carpenter. The carpenter is made by two parents. And on it goes. But who or what caused the very first thing that ever happened? God.
3. *Nothing comes from nothing.* All physical things have a beginning and an end. Nothing cannot cause something. So, before anything else existed, who or what made the very first thing ever made? God.
4. *More or less.* Objects and people in the world have different amounts of certain qualities, such as goodness. But we can only decide more or less goodness by comparing our goodness to the maximum goodness. And who is maximum goodness? God.
5. *The Director.* Things in the world move toward specific goals. Day moves toward night, and winter moves toward spring, just as an arrow moves toward a target because the archer aimed it there. So, there must be an intelligent being who directs all things in the world to their proper goals. Who is that? God.

   These five proofs were developed by St. Thomas Aquinas between A.D. 1200–1300.

God Creates the World	Noah and the Flood	The Tower of Babel

CREATION	3000–2500 B.C.	2400 B.C.
Chariots used in Mesopotamia	3000 B.C.—The site of Athens is inhabited by this time in present day Greece.	2686 B.C.—The Egyptian Old Kingdom begins. 2650 B.C.—The Step Pyramid of King Zoser, the oldest pyramid is built.

3000–2500 B.C.

The Great Flood

Genesis 6–9

History & Politics

2600 B.C. Yucatan Peninsula. The Mayan civilization was set up and growing about this time.

Literature & Theater

Sumer. Pepi's papyrus entitled "Instructions to a Son" was written. This is one of the earliest works of literature that has been saved.

*A*fter God had to put Adam and Eve out of the Garden of Eden, people became more and more evil. Almost 1,650 years passed after the world had been created. During that time people became so evil that God sadly decided he had to destroy the world he had made. The people he loved had stopped loving him—everyone, that is, except a man named Noah.

Noah was a good man who loved God with all his heart. He and his family obeyed God's commands. The Bible says "Noah walked with God," just as Adam and Eve had walked with him in the garden before they sinned. So God decided to save Noah's family. He told Noah and his sons to build a huge boat (called an "ark") because he was going to flood the whole world with water and drown every living thing that wasn't on the boat. So Noah and his sons built the boat exactly as God told them.

24

Building the Boat

The boat was gigantic! In fact, it was longer than a football field and had three stories (called "decks"). It was made out of gopher wood—a special kind of wood God told them to use. And it had a window that ran along under the roof all the way around the top of the boat. It also had one big door where people, animals, and supplies could be put on the boat.

It took many months for Noah and his sons to build the boat. But it was finally finished. Then God sent a pair of each kind of animal and bird in the world to Noah to be saved from the flood. He sent seven pairs of some special kinds of birds and animals. After the flood was over, these animals and birds would have babies and fill up the earth again.

HISTORY MYSTERY

What musical instruments could Noah's family have taken with them onto the boat?

Answer: Small harp and flute.

Religion, Philosophy & Learning

Sumer and Egypt. Schools are set up to teach reading and writing to boys.

Visual Arts

Egypt. The great sphinx of Giza was built. The Egyptians thought it guarded the pyramids. It was one of the forms of their false god of the sun. Its face may have looked like Khafre, the king of Egypt.

Music

China. The first bamboo musical pipe was made by Linglun, a famous musician who played in the Chinese courts.

Science, Technology & Growth

2500 B.C. Europe. The weaving loom was first known to be used by European women.

Daily Life

- Dogs were first tamed for pets.

- 2600 B.C. Egypt. Pancakes were first eaten.
- 2500 B.C. Peru. Cotton was first cultivated for cloth.
- Metal coins were first used.
- Egypt. Mirrors were first developed.

Get on Board!

Noah, his family, and all the animals got on the boat. Then God himself closed the big door. And it started to rain. It rained for forty days and nights! Water also came up from springs in the ground. Finally, the whole world was covered with water, even the mountains were twenty feet under water! Every person, every animal, and every bird that had lived on earth died, except for those on the boat with Noah.

The people and animals stayed on the boat for over a year. At long last, the water went away and the land dried out. Then Noah, his family, and God's zoo came off the boat to a brand new world that was clean and good, just as God had created the world the first time. God had taken care of the people he loved and who loved him.

DID YOU KNOW THAT...

Noah and his family might have eaten popcorn on the ark? Popcorn had been a popular food for many years by that time.

God's Promise

Then God made an agreement with Noah. He promised that he would never again destroy the entire earth with a flood, no matter how evil people became. Suddenly the first rainbow appeared in the sky. God said the rainbow will appear when it rains, and when he sees it he will remember his agreement not to destroy the entire earth with water. Today, when we see a rainbow, we know that God is taking care of the people he loves and those of us who love him.

"Noah did everything that God commanded him. "

Genesis 6:22

BIBLE MYSTERY

What bird announced that the Flood was over? (See Genesis 8:12.)
Answer: Dove

The Epic of Gilgamesh

Several different ancient writings, besides the Bible, tell the story of a great flood. The Epic of Gilgamesh is one of those stories and has become an important work of literature. It was written on clay tablets about 2000 B.C. Here is the story of this epic poem.

Gilgamesh was a cruel king in Babylon. According to the myth, the Babylonian false gods heard the prayers of the people of the city of Ereck (which is now Warka, Iraq), who were being mistreated. They sent a wild, mean man named Enkidu to fight Gilgamesh. The fight ended when neither man could win, and Gilgamesh and Enkidu became close friends. They traveled together, shared many adventures, and became famous.

When the two travelers returned to Ereck, the false goddess Ishtar announced her love for Gilgamesh. When he rejected her, she sent the mythical Bull of Heaven to destroy Ereck. Gilgamesh and Enkidu killed the bull, and, the false gods killed Enkidu in return. Then Gilgamesh asked a wise man named Utnapishtim for the secret of living forever. The wise man told Gilgamesh the story about a great flood. Its details are very close to the story in the Bible. The wise man also told Gilgamesh that a plant of eternal youth was in the sea. Gilgamesh dived into the water and found the plant, but later he lost it to a serpent. Sad and lonely, Gilgamesh returned to Ereck where he lived out his life.

Noah and the Flood	The Tower of Babel	Abraham/ Isaac— Born and Sacrificed
3000–2500 B.C.	2400 B.C.	2091–2066 B.C.

2500 B.C.—Corn is domesti-
cated in Mesoamerica.

2500 B.C.—The city of Ur
becomes the capital of Sumer.

2300 B.C.—The
Hittites enter
Anatolia.

2133 B.C.—Egypt is reunited during the 11th dynasty of the
Middle Kingdom.

2400 B.C. What Did You Say?

Genesis 11:1–9

History & Politics

China. The famous Yangshao dynasty ended about this time in history.

*D*id you ever wonder why there are so many different languages in the world? Why can't everyone just speak the same language, and all our problems would be over, right? That's not what God thought.

After God had saved his people from the flood, they began to have children and become a bigger and bigger nation. And, once again, as they grew larger, they forgot about God, his love for them, and how much they needed him. Sin and evil came back into the world, and people no longer obeyed God's commands.

The Tower of Babel

A s the people moved east, they settled in the Plain of Shinar in Babylon. There they decided to build a great city with a tower so high they said it would "reach the heavens." This meant they didn't feel they needed God anymore. They thought they could reach heaven without his help.

The people also wanted to make a name for themselves or become famous. They thought if they worked together, they could do anything they wanted to do... without God's help.

At that time, all people in the whole world spoke the same language. But God didn't like the way they were thinking. They were too proud of their

Literature & Theater

Mesopotamia. The first known libraries were built.

Religion, Philosophy & Learning

Crete. The snake and the bull were religious symbols being used by the Minoan people.

Visual Arts

China. Painted and black pottery were being made about this same time.

Music

Sumer. The bull lyre was one of the musical instruments played for entertainment at this time. It was often decorated with pictures of animals, such as a wolf, lion, donkey, bear, deer, or goat.

Science, Technology & Growth

2400 B.C. Egypt. The people of Egypt first developed and began using papyrus for writing paper. This was a major step forward in science, literature, and other areas of learning because it was much easier to keep records.

Daily Life

- 2350 b.c. Mesopotamia. The first toilet was built in the Akkadian palace at Eshnunna.
- Babylon. The first chickens were tamed.
- 2600 b.c. India. Farmers first began using the plow to till their land.
- Egypt. Dog racing was popular with the Egyptian people. It's still popular today!

own abilities and had forgotten him. So he decided to remind people of how much they needed him and to make them depend on him again.

Language Becomes Confused

God went down to the tower, which was probably built like an ancient ziggurat, and confused the language of the people building it. In other words, they all started speaking different languages and couldn't understand each other anymore. When they could no longer talk to each other, they stopped building the tower. Then they moved away to different parts of the world to settle in groups with other people who spoke the same languages they did.

Mind Meld

"That is where the Lord confused the language of the whole world. So the place is called Babel."

Genesis 11:9

The city and tower that the people had begun to build was named Babel, which sounds like the Hebrew word for confused. Today, when someone is talking nonsense, we sometimes say, "Oh, stop your babbling."

Anytime we forget that God is in control of our lives, we start babbling, too.

So, when you hear someone speaking a different language than your own, remember that God wants us to depend on him and his grace to get to heaven. We can't get there on our own.

The first great libraries were built in Mesopotamia about this same time.

What Is a Ziggurat?

Ziggurats were temples to local false gods in early Bible times. They existed several hundred years before the first pyramid was built in Egypt, and they were as tall as the pyramids.

Ziggurats had either four or seven different levels. Each level was slightly smaller than the one below it. Stairs angled up each level of the temple, eventually leading to the top level, where the main room, called the cella, was found. It was in this main room that sacrifices were made to the false gods.

The most famous ziggurat of all was the Tower of Babel, described in this Bible story. The Jews thought that the Tower of Babel was located at Nimrud.

Since ziggurats were temples to local false gods, is it any wonder that God didn't want the people he loved building one?

BIBLE MYSTERY
Since there were many languages in the world after God confused them, in what language was the Old Testament originally written?
Answer: Hebrew

31

2333 B.C.—Legendary figure Tangun is said to have established the first Korean kingdom.

2133 B.C.—Egypt is reunited during the 11th dynasty of the Middle Kingdom.

2000 B.C.—The Celts emerge in Europe.

2000 B.C.—Megalith stone alignments are erected at Carnac in present-day France.

2091–2066 B.C. The Nations Begin

Genesis 12–23

History & Politics

Egypt. The Pharaohs began ruling as the kings (and one queen) of Egypt.

Literature & Theater

Babylon. Poems were written celebrating the creation of the world.

When the people left Babel and moved to all parts of the world, families got together to form clans, clans formed tribes, and tribes combined to form nations. Each of us descended from one of these great nations.

Chosen to Serve

One nation was made up of Hebrew people, who were descendants of Noah and his son, Shem. The Hebrew nation is talked about in the Bible more than any other nation because God chose it to serve a very special purpose. After Adam and Eve sinned, God put his plan into motion to save his people from their sins and bring them back to him. He planned to send his Son Jesus into the world to save the people he loved so much. But first, he had to prepare the world for Jesus. And he needed a pure nation into which Jesus could be born. He chose the Hebrews to be that nation.

After the Hebrews were chosen by God for this special job, the Old Testament doesn't tell much about the other nations in the world. (The stories of those nations are told in other world history books.) The Bible mostly records the story of the Hebrew people preparing for Jesus' coming. God used this great family to keep his worship and truth pure. Through them God blessed the whole world with Jesus because he loves us all so deeply.

God's Promise

About eight generations after Shem lived, Abram was born in the Hebrew nation. When Abram grew to be a man, God called him to be the father of the Hebrews, and he promised Abram that all the nations of the earth would be blessed

---

BIBLE MYSTERY
How could a 100-year-old man become the father of a whole nation?
Answer: By the power and promise of God.

Religion, Philosophy & Learning

Egypt. The Isis and Osiris cult, who believed in the resurrection of the dead, was established.

Visual Arts

Egypt. The Saqqara pyramids were built.

Science, Technology & Growth

The bow and arrow is known to have been used in warfare.

through him and his children. Then he changed Abram's name to Abraham, which means "honored father of many."

Abraham and his wife, Sarah, grew very old, but they still had no children. Was God going to keep his promise? Finally, when Abraham was one hundred years old, and Sarah was ninety years old, they had a baby boy named Isaac. At last it seemed that God was keeping his promise to make Abraham the father of a great nation. But one day when Isaac was a young man, God told Abraham to take Isaac and offer his son as a sacrifice to him. Abraham didn't under-

Daily Life

Yucatan Peninsula. The Mayan people were planting maize and worshiping a false god of maize.

The Lord said to Abram,
"… I will make you a great nation…
all the people on earth will be blessed
through you. "

Genesis 12:1–3

DID YOU KNOW THAT...

the Hebrews
of Abraham's time
are the same people
we call Jews today?

stand why God asked him to sacrifice Isaac, but he trusted God completely, and he did as God had told him to do. Just as he was about to kill Isaac for the sacrifice, an angel stopped him.

Because Abraham did not keep his only son from God, he was blessed greatly by God and became the father of millions of Hebrew people down through the ages. God always keeps his promises to the people he loves.

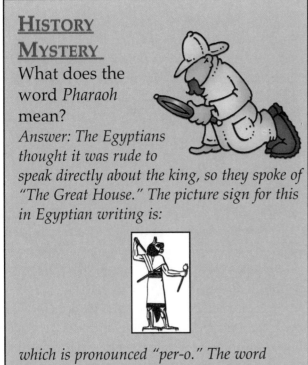

Legend of the Minotaur Monster

History is filled with imaginary legends and fairy tales. One famous legend is about the Minotaur Monster.

To the ancient people of Greece, the island of Crete was a place of legend and mystery. They believed that Crete was once ruled by a powerful king named King Minos. One Crete legend was about a famous Greek hero named Theseus, who traveled to the palace of King Minos. In the huge basement of the palace, where there were many rooms and hallways, Theseus was said to have met and killed the terrible Minotaur Monster. The legend claimed that the monster was half man and half bull, and that King Minos was his father.

No one really took the legend seriously . Then, in the early 1900s, Arthur Evans—a British archaeologist—began to dig around the city of Knossos on Crete. And he found the remains of a huge palace, with a complex system of rooms and hallways in the basement. Later, more palaces and towns were found on Crete. Then they were sure that a rich and powerful nation existed there thousands of years before.

Arthur Evans named the newly found ancient civilization "Minoan," after the legendary King Minos. Since then we have discovered many other things about the Minoans and how they lived.

While the story of the Minotaur Monster was only fiction, the people who first told the legend were certainly real.

Abraham/Isaac—Born
and Sacrificed

Jacob & Esau
Are Born

Twelve Tribes of Israel
Joseph in Egypt

2091 B.C.

2066 B.C.

1885 B.C.

2133 B.C.—Egypt is reunited
during the 11th dynasty of
the Middle kingdom.

2000 B.C.—The Akkadian
poem, the Epic of
Gilgamesh is composed.

2000 B.C.—The Celts emerge
in Europe.

1991 B.C.—Amenemhet
I overthrows the
Theban rulers of
Egypt to found the
12th Dynasty.

1900 B.C.—The
Assyrians are
unified during
the Old Assyr-
ian period.

Twin Nations Are Born

2066 B.C. *Genesis 25–28*

History & Politics

- 2100–1700 B.C. Egypt. The old kingdom ended, and the middle kingdom began.
- World population was about 27 million people.

Literature & Theater

Egypt. Writings and literature discussed the meaning of life.

*W*hen we think about God's "chosen people," we often think that they were amazing, superhuman people, don't we? We may think they were chosen because they were special people. But the Hebrew nation was full of ordinary people, just like us, who were chosen for a special job.

Sometimes God's chosen people did things the right way; sometimes they made mistakes. Sometimes they worshiped and served God as he asked; sometimes they forgot about God and turned to the false gods of nations around them. They often sinned against God, but then they changed their hearts and lives and came back to him.

Whether the Hebrew people obeyed God perfectly or not, they still had a special job to do. And God, who loved them so much, helped them do it. He was always protecting them, correcting them, and leading them toward their goal of bringing Jesus into the world.

Isaac, the New Leader

After Abraham died, his son Isaac became leader of the Hebrew people. Isaac was very much like his father. He did some of the same things well, and he made some of the same mistakes his father had made.

When Isaac was forty years old, he married Rebekah, and they had twin boys named Esau and Jacob. God told Rebekah that her two sons would be leaders of two different nations some day. He said that when they grew up, the baby born first would serve the baby born second. That meant that Esau's nation would have to serve Jacob's nation. But that seemed strange to Rebekah and Isaac because Hebrew custom said that the son born first should

A Surprise Disguise!

Esau was a hairy man. Jacob put goatskins on his smooth hands and neck and tricked his father Isaac, who couldn't see, into thinking he was Esau and giving him the blessing that went with Esau's birthright.
See Genesis 27:1–40

Religion, Philosophy & Learning

The false goddess Ishtar was worshiped as the goddess of love.

Visual Arts

Sumer. Sumeric-Akkadian art was at its height.

Music

2000 B.C. Denmark. The first trumpets were reported being played in Denmark.

Science, Technology & Growth

- South America. Potatoes and sweet potatoes were discovered.
- 2000 B.C. Mesopotamia. Spoked wheels on chariots were being used.

Daily Life

2000 B.C.

- Mesopotamia. Horses were used to pull chariots and carts with wheels.
- Egypt. Clay Lydia balls were probably the first children's toys. Jacob and Esau may have played with them as children.
- Africa. Watermelons were first cultivated.
- China. Ice cream was invented when a soft milk-and-rice mixture was packed in snow.
- India. Bananas and tea were first cultivated.

become the family leader after the father died. It was called a birthright. In other words, the oldest son had certain rights because his birth came first.

The Trade

Esau was a hunter, and Jacob was a farmer. One day Esau came home from hunting, and he was very hungry. Jacob had been making some stew, so Esau begged Jacob to let him have some of the stew. Jacob offered to trade Esau some stew for his birthright. Esau was so hungry that he didn't act wisely; he agreed to the trade. And that's how God's promise to Rebekah came true. Esau, who was

The Lord said to Rebekah, "… two groups of people will be taken from you… The older will serve the younger. "

Genesis 25:23

older, had to serve his younger brother Jacob because Jacob owned the birthright.

Why was that so important? When Isaac died, Jacob, not Esau, became the leader of the Hebrew nation, and it was through that nation–God's chosen people–that Jesus was born into the world. Esau had given up his right to give the world its Savior.

BIBLE MYSTERY

"CASE OF THE UNFORGETTABLE SOUP"

See if you can figure out this Bible mystery by using the clues below.

Clue #1: Esau ended up "in the soup" because of this.

Clue #2: Esau's was worth twice as much as Jacob's.

Clue #3: Genesis 25:27–34.

Answer: Birthright.

Babylon: City of Wonder

The people of Babylon were the most powerful in Asia until about 2000 B.C. They led the world in writing, language, and literature. They were the first to discover and invent tools and objects that would make work easier, such as the wheel, the plow, and the oil-burning lamp.

Babylon was one of the greatest cities of Isaac's time. Its walls were 350 feet high! They were also 87 feet wide, which was wide enough for six chariots to race side by side.

Babylon had over 100 gates, and they were all made of polished bronze. One of its palaces covered more than 11 acres inside the walls. And one banquet hall seated over 10,000 people!

The walls of the city were covered with hand-painted enamel tiles, which pictured events from Babylon's history.

Babylon's land was good for raising crops and animals. And the city was the center of major world trade. It was truly a wonder to see!

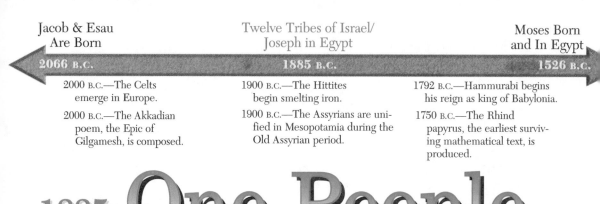

Jacob & Esau Are Born	Twelve Tribes of Israel/ Joseph in Egypt	Moses Born and In Egypt
2066 B.C.	1885 B.C.	1526 B.C.

2000 B.C.—The Celts emerge in Europe.

2000 B.C.—The Akkadian poem, the Epic of Gilgamesh, is composed.

1900 B.C.—The Hittites begin smelting iron.

1900 B.C.—The Assyrians are unified in Mesopotamia during the Old Assyrian period.

1792 B.C.—Hammurabi begins his reign as king of Babylonia.

1750 B.C.—The Rhind papyrus, the earliest surviving mathematical text, is produced.

1885 B.C. One People, Twelve Tribes

History & Politics

1800–1750 B.C. Babylon. Hammurabi, King of Babylonia, reunited the kingdom. He developed the famous sets of laws called the

Code of Hammurabi. These laws governed family, civil matters, crime, and business. They are the basis for many of our laws today.

Literature & Theater

- Egypt. The first novel, titled *Story of Sinuhe*, was written.
- 1900 B.C. Crete. Script writing for plays first began.

Genesis 29–50

*J*ust as God had told Isaac and Rebekah, their younger son, Jacob, became leader of the Hebrew people after Isaac died. Esau's family, the Edomite nation, often served or fought the Hebrews, as God had said.

Tricked!

During his travels, Jacob visited his uncle Laban, who had two daughters, Leah (the older one) and Rachel. While there, Jacob fell in love with Rachel and offered to work seven years in trade for Rachel to become his wife. Laban agreed to the plan, but when it came time for the wedding, Laban gave Leah to Jacob instead.

When Jacob discovered that he had been tricked, he became upset and went to see Laban, who said that their custom did not allow a younger daughter to marry before the older one. Laban offered to give Rachel to Jacob, too, if he would then work another seven years to pay for her. Because Jacob loved Rachel, he agreed. So, in all, Jacob worked fourteen years for Rachel.

Through the years, Jacob became the father of twelve sons and one daughter. His twelve sons later became leaders of twelve large tribes within the Hebrew nation. Rachel was the mother of two of Jacob's sons—Joseph and Benjamin. And because Joseph was Rachel's first son, he was Jacob's favorite.

Sold into Slavery

Joseph's brothers were jealous of Jacob's special love for Joseph. So, one day they

> ### HISTORY MYSTERY
> Who built Stonehenge in England, and why did they build it?
> *Answer: Scholars are uncertain about who built Stonehenge, but many think it was built by the Druids as a temple to their false god.*

Religion, Philosophy & Learning

- England. Stonehenge, an ancient stone circle, was completed. It was probably a temple to a false god, but some scholars think it was also used as a calendar.

It may have taken about a thousand men to move one of the giant stones into place.

- Babylon. Marduk became the false god they worshiped.

Visual Arts

Britain and Western Europe. Artists began working with bronze. This time period was called "The Bronze Age."

Music

Egypt. Percussion instruments, such as drums, began to be used in Egyptian orchestra music.

Science, Technology & Growth

- Egypt. Mercury was first discovered and used.
- India. Scientists discovered and named four of the basic elements: earth, air, fire, and water.
- 1800 B.C. Babylon. Medical instruments were first invented and used.

Daily Life

- Middle East. Apples were cultivated and eaten.
- Babylon. The kings of Babylonia began the custom of shaking hands.
- China. The sport of falconry was practiced.

grabbed Joseph and sold him to a caravan of people going to Egypt. Then they made their father believe that Joseph had been killed by a wild animal.

In Egypt, Joseph was protected and blessed by God. He became popular with the king (pharaoh), and after a few years was given the second most important job in the country. As God would have it, a famine (when no food grows) happened in Joseph's homeland, and Jacob sent his ten older sons to Egypt to buy food. Because Joseph ruled over the sale of

Joseph said, "You meant to hurt me. But God turned your evil into good. It was to save the lives of many people. And it is being done."

Genesis 50:20

BIBLE MYSTERY
How could a Hebrew slave boy become ruler of the nation that captured him?
Answer: Joseph became ruler of Egypt because it was part of God's plan to save the people he loved.

Dɪᴅ ʏᴏᴜ ᴋɴᴏᴡ ᴛʜᴀᴛ...

God helped Joseph tell
the king of Egypt
what his dream meant?
Then Joseph was taken
out of prison and made
Egypt's prime minister!
See Genesis 41

food in Egypt, his brothers had to come to him for the food. When they saw that it was Joseph, they were afraid he would kill them for what they had done to him years before.

Good for Evil

Joseph said, "You meant to hurt me. But God turned your evil into good." Then he hugged his brothers and sent them home to bring Jacob, Benjamin, and his whole family to live in Egypt where there was plenty of food and land. Once again God had taken care of the people he loved and who loved him.

Who Invented the ABCs?

Our alphabet is very important to us. If we didn't have the letters in our alphabet, you couldn't be reading this book! I couldn't be writing it. And there would be no Bible to tell us about God and his people. But where did our alphabet come from? Who invented it?

About 1700 B.C. the first alphabet was invented in a country called Phoenicia (fo-NEE-shah). The first written characters stood for simple sounds, rather than for whole words.

Several nations made up their own methods of writing, but the people of Phoenicia came up with the first real alphabet, which had twenty-two letters in it. It looked like the letters under "Phoenician," below.

After that, the people of Greece took the alphabet of Phoenicia and developed it even further into their own set of letters. It was so simple to use that many people learned to read and write. See the letters under "Greek."

Finally, the Latin people, such as the people of Italy, improved on the Greek alphabet. This Latin alphabet is the one used by many countries in the world today, including ours. It looks like the letters under "English."

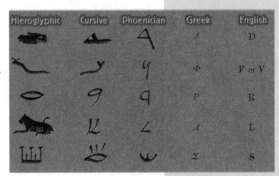

Hieroglyphic	Cursive	Phoenician	Greek	English
		A	A	D
		ꟼ	Φ	F or V
		ꟼ	P	R
		∠	A	L
		ꞷ	Σ	S

Twelve Tribes of Israel/
Joseph in Egypt

Moses Born and
In Egypt

God Delivers Israel
from Egypt

1885 B.C.

1526 B.C.

1446 B.C.

1766 B.C.—The Shang dynasty
begins in the Hwang Ho
valley in China.

1700 B.C.—The palaces at
Knossos and Phaistos on
Crete are destroyed by fire.

1570 B.C.—Egyptian expansion
begins under the New
Kingdom pharaohs.

1550 B.C.—Assyria becomes part
of the Kingdom of Mitanni.

1500 B.C.—Glassmaking
is perfected in Egypt
and the Near East.

1500 B.C.—The Phoenicians
found the city of Tangier
in North Africa.

1526 B.C.

Pauper, Prince, and Prophet

Exodus 1–6

History & Politics

- Babylon. The Babylonian Empire started to decline under the leadership of Hammurabi's son, Samsuiluna.
  - 1503 B.C. Egypt. Queen Hatshepsut became the only woman to rule Egypt as Pharaoh.
  - 1512 B.C. Egypt. Thutmose I was the first pharaoh to be buried in the Valley of the Kings.

Literature & Theater

- 1500–600 B.C. China. The first of seven periods of Chinese literature.
- 1500 B.C. The Book of Job in the Bible may have been written.

A few years after Joseph's family moved to Egypt, the King of Egypt died, and a new king began to rule. This new king didn't know Joseph or what he had done for Egypt.

By this time, the people of Jacob (also called Israel), had many children and had become a strong nation. Egypt was filled with them. The new king became afraid that they would leave Egypt, and the Egyptians would no longer have slaves to work for them. So the king made life hard for the people of Israel. Slave masters forced them to make bricks, build cities, and work in the fields. Still, Israel grew stronger.

At last the king commanded that all boy babies born to Israel be drowned in the Nile River. One Hebrew family had a baby boy named Moses. His mother hid him from the king for three months. Then she made a basket of reeds and tar, put him in it, and placed the basket-bed in the Nile River.

From Pauper to Prince

Soon the king's daughter came to the river to take a bath. She found the tiny basket-boat and looked inside. Baby Moses was crying, and she felt sorry for him. So she adopted him herself, and took him home to the palace. Moses grew up with the best food, clothes, education, and training. He was a prince of Egypt!

One day Moses saw an Egyptian man beating a Hebrew slave. Moses killed the Egyptian. Then he ran away from Egypt so that the king wouldn't kill him for what he had done. He went to Midian where he lived with a man named Jethro and his family.

Religion, Philosophy & Learning

- 1700 B.C. The religion of Judaism was begun.
- Egypt. A collection of religious documents called *The Book of the Dead* was put together to guide the dead on their spiritual journey.

- 1500–600 B.C. India. The Hindu religion was begun. This religion worships false gods and is based on the caste system, which ranks people according to their religious practices, employment, where they live, and other things. Today there are about 648 million people who belong to this false religion.

HISTORY MYSTERY

The Hebrews and the Egyptians were enemies, but the King of Egypt's daughter helped the Hebrews. Why?

Answer: She didn't know she was saving the Hebrew leader-to-be. And she was doing what God wanted her to do, even though she didn't know it.

Music

Egypt. The kithara (KITH-uh-ruh) was developed. This wooden instrument is a larger version of the lyre. It is supported by a strap and played by plucking its strings with a pick. Moses surely heard this instrument played in the palace of the King of Egypt.

Science, Technology & Growth

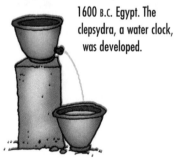

1600 B.C. Egypt. The clepsydra, a water clock, was developed.

From Prince to Prophet

After many years, the King of Egypt died. The people of Israel prayed for God to rescue them from their slavery, and God heard his people's cry for help.

One day Moses saw something very strange. A bush was on fire, but it wasn't burning up. As he stepped closer, he heard a voice say, "Moses." It was the voice of God! God told Moses that he wanted him to go to Egypt and lead his people out of slavery.

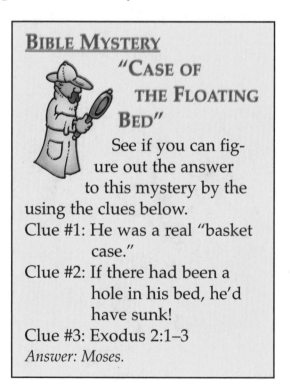

BIBLE MYSTERY

"CASE OF THE FLOATING BED"

See if you can figure out the answer to this mystery by the using the clues below.

Clue #1: He was a real "basket case."

Clue #2: If there had been a hole in his bed, he'd have sunk!

Clue #3: Exodus 2:1–3

Answer: Moses.

Moses tried to talk God out of sending him to Egypt, but God knew that Moses was perfect for the job. God had made sure that Moses grew up in the king's own palace, spoke the Egyptian language, and had all the right training. Finally, Moses agreed to go and rescue God's people, and God promised to help him every step of the way.

Mind Meld

"So the Israelites believed. They heard that the Lord was concerned about them and had seen their troubles. Then they bowed down and worshiped him."

Exodus 4:31

The Art of Making Glass

Glassmaking is a very special artistic skill. And making glass has been around for thousands of years.

3000 B.C. Decorative glass was first made in about 3000 B.C. in Egypt and Mesopotamia. The first glass objects may have been made to look like gems. But since glassmaking was very costly in those days, making glass look like gems may have been as expensive as the real gems were. Early Egyptian glassmakers probably made simple glass beads.

1500 B.C. About 1500 years after the Egyptians learned to make glass, about the time of Moses, people in Egypt, Greece, and Phoenicia learned how to make bottles and other glass containers. They dipped a sand-filled cloth bag into a vat of melted glass, which coated the bag and took the bag's shape. When the glass cooled, the sand was emptied out, and the bag was pulled out, leaving a glass bottle or jar. The Hebrew people may have learned how to make glass while they were slaves in Egypt.

100 B.C. Glassmakers in Syria developed a less costly way of making glass. They put a blob of melted glass on the end of a long pipe and then blew air through the other end of the pipe. The air formed a bubble inside the glass that could be shaped to make bottles and other open containers.

High-quality, fine glass pieces are still made by glassblowers today. Then glass etchers and designers cut beautiful patterns and pictures into the finished bottles, bowls, and other pieces. This expensive kind of glass is made at such places as the Waterford Crystal Factory in Ireland.

DID YOU KNOW THAT...

Moses wrote the first five books of the Bible? They are called "The Pentateuch." The books are Genesis, Exodus, Leviticus, Numbers, and Deuteronomy.

Moses Born and
In Egypt

God Delivers Israel
from Egypt

God Gives Moses the
Ten Commandments

1526 B.C.

1446 B.C.

1445 B.C.

1503 B.C.—Queen Hatshepsut
becomes the only woman
to rule Egypt as pharaoh.

1500 B.C.—Writing of the Hindu
Vedas begin in India.

1450 B.C.—Minoan civilization on Crete is overrun
by invaders from the
Greek mainland.

1400 B.C.—Anyang
becomes the
capital of the
Shang dynasty.

1446 B.C.

Pharaohs & Plagues

Exodus 7–12

From Mt. Sinai (SY-ny), also known as "the mountain of God," where Moses had seen the burning bush, he and his brother Aaron went to the leaders of Israel and told them all that God had said. They showed Israel some powerful miracles God had given them to use in rescuing Israel from Egypt, and the people believed. And when the people heard that God was sad about their troubles, they bowed down and worshiped him.

Facing Off with Pharaoh

After that, Moses and Aaron went to see the King of Egypt, called Pharaoh. They said, "This is what the Lord, the God of Israel says: 'Let my people go so they may hold a feast for me in the desert.' "

History & Politics

Mexico. The earliest known settlement in Mexico was established. It was called Chiapa de Carzo.

Chiapa de Carzo

Literature & Theater

The Bible books of Genesis, Exodus, and Numbers were probably written.

Religion, Philosophy & Learning

1600–1450 B.C. Crete. The false snake goddess was worshiped and known as the "mother goddess." Three snakes wound around her body and headdress. Some people believe the statue was of a queen or a priestess snake handler. This false religious belief may have come from Mesopotamia.

Visual Arts

Crete. The famous Cretan terra-cotta vases were first made.

But Pharaoh refused to let them go and sent Moses and Aaron away. Then he ordered the slave masters to make Israel work even harder than before.

So God said to Moses, "Now you will see what I will do to the king of Egypt. I will use my great power against him, and he will let my people go."

Then God caused ten different plagues (disasters) to happen to Egypt, one after the other, in order to force Pharaoh to let the people of Israel leave their slavery. Each time the plague hurt the people of Egypt, but it did not hurt the people of Israel, because God loved and protected his own people. (See the side column for a description of the plagues.)

Each time a plague came upon Egypt, Pharaoh would agree to let Israel leave. But when God stopped the plague, then Pharaoh would not keep his promise, and he wouldn't let Israel go.

Passover

Finally came the tenth plague, and God went through the land of Egypt and killed the oldest son of each Egyptian family, including the son of Pharaoh. But Israel was not harmed because all the people followed God's command to eat a special meal called Passover and to put lamb's blood above their doors. In the Passover meal they ate roasted lamb to

Music

The Hittites first developed and played the guitar.

Science, Technology & Growth

It's possible that a first Suez Canal existed.

Daily Life

- Egypt and India. Leprosy—the name for several different harmful skin diseases—was identified.
- 1500 B.C. Various countries. Wooden spoons were invented and in use.

The Lord said, "I have seen the troubles my people have suffered in Egypt… am concerned about their pain."

Exodus 3:7

The Ten Plagues

1. Water turned to blood in all the rivers of Egypt (Exodus 7:14–24).
2. Frogs covered the land of Egypt (Exodus 8:1–15).
3. Storms of pesky gnats invaded Egypt (Exodus 8:16–19).
4. Hordes of flies swarmed over the people of Egypt (Exodus 8:20–32).
5. The Egyptian farm animals all came down with a disease (Exodus 9:1–7).
6. Painful boils covered the skin of all the Egyptian people (Exodus 9: 8–12).
7. Fierce hail hammered the homes and crops of Egypt (Exodus 9:13–35).
8. Millions of locusts attacked the crops and houses of Egypt (Exodus 10:1–20).
9. Thick darkness covered Egypt night and day (Exodus 10:21–29).
10. The firstborn son of every Egyptian family was killed (Exodus 11).

honor God because he passed over their homes without killing their children.

Then Pharaoh said to Moses and Aaron, "Get up and leave my people. You and your people may do as you have asked. Go and worship the Lord. And hurry! If you don't, we will all die!"

The Exodus

That same night, exactly 430 years after they came to Egypt, the people of Israel left Egypt. About 600,000 men, along with the women and children, left Egypt together. They took rich gifts of gold and silver with them from their Egyptian neighbors. And they took a large number of sheep, goats, and cattle.

That night, God led his people out of slavery and into

BIBLE MYSTERY

Who had a hair-raising experience?

Answer: Eliphaz, one of Job's friends. A spirit floated past his face one night in a dream. Eliphaz was so scared that the hair on his body stood on end. See Job 4:12–15.

freedom. Every year after that the people of Israel celebrated the Passover Feast and remembered how God rescued them from their enemies.

It's a FACT!

Some scholars believe that when Israel left Egypt, counting men, women, children, and other people who went with them, about 2,000,000 people escaped!

Ancient Games and Sports

Just as we enjoy sports and games today, ancient people also liked them. But their games and sports were very different than ours are today.

Many of the sporting events and athletic games in ancient times were held in honor of false gods, and some were held as offerings of thanksgiving to them. The games were both a religious and a social activity. Other games, in later times, were held in honor of living persons.

Greece. The athletic games in Greece also had parades, feasts, and music. (Does that sound a little like our football games where we have concession stands and bands playing?) In the early years of Greek games, the players were ordinary citizens. Later more and more professional athletes participated in the games. But the more professional the Greek games became, the less popular they were with the people.

Rome. The Roman games were very different than the Greek games. In Rome, the people only watched the games, rather than playing in them. Only professional athletes, slaves, and prisoners played in the games. The Roman games were also cruel and violent. They often staged battles fought to the death between large numbers of people and animals.

God delivers Israel
from Egypt

God Gives Moses
the Ten Commandments

The Promised Land
Is Conquered

1446 B.C.

1445 B.C.

1406–1400 B.C.

1450 B.C.—The Mycenaeans
dominate the Aegean.

1450 B.C.—The Minoan civilization on
Crete is overrun by Greek invaders
from the mainland.

1400 B.C.—Anyang becomes
the capital of the Shang
dynasty.

1400 B.C.—The city of Ravenna is
founded by Italic tribes.

1445 B.C. An Agreement with God

*Exodus
13–40*

History & Politics

Egypt. Trade with other countries and
Egyptian culture was strong.

With a shout of joy, the people of Israel left
Egypt and started out for the Red Sea. They
were free! Suddenly Pharaoh panicked. All the
slaves had escaped. So he gathered his entire army
and chased after Israel. He finally caught up to the
people of Israel at the Red Sea.

A Path to Safety

The people of Israel were terrified.
Egypt was behind them, and the Red
Sea was in front of them. What would
they do? Moses told them to stand still
and watch the power of God. Moses
stretched out his walking stick over the
sea, and God made a strong wind blow to
form a dry pathway through the sea.
Then the people of Israel walked through

the Red Sea on dry ground, with a wall of water on each side of them. Amazing! Pharaoh's soldiers tried to follow Israel through the sea, but God caused the water to collapse around them, and they all drowned. God had saved his people again.

From the Red Sea, Israel traveled about three months to Mt. Sinai, where Moses had first seen the burning bush.

The Agreement

About 635 years has passed since God promised Abraham that all nations would be blessed through him. But the time had finally come for God to keep his promise.

Literature & Theater

- China. The first Chinese dictionary was published with over 40,000 characters.

- The Book of Leviticus in the Bible was probably written between 1446–1406 B.C.

Visual Arts

Egypt. Fancy tapestries were first made.

Music

Egypt. Harp music was being played for court dances.

Science, Technology & Growth

China. The famous "Magic Squares" were developed in Chinese mathematics.

Daily Life

China. Silk cloth was being made, which eventually caused increased trade all over the world.

So he came down to Mt. Sinai to renew his Agreement with Abraham's family—Israel.

Until then, everyone had lived under God's law of good versus evil. The other nations would continue living under that law, but God would give Israel a new law—a special law just for them. This law would keep Israel pure and holy, ready to receive God's Son Jesus.

Israel was excited about God's Agreement, but the people didn't know how hard it would be to keep. Moses went up on Mt. Sinai, and the people waited at the foot of the mountain. God wrote ten laws with his own finger onto two stone tablets and gave them to

DID YOU KNOW THAT...

God actually wrote the Ten Commandments on stone twice? Moses broke the first stone tablets because the people had made a false god and were worshiping it. See Exodus 32:15–20; 34:27–28.

Moses. We call them the Ten Commandments. He also gave Moses over 600 other laws for Israel to follow during the next forty years. We call these the Law of Moses.

Among the laws God gave Moses were directions on how to build a Holy Tent (also called the Tabernacle) for God. The Holy Tent was where God himself would live among the people he loved. It would always be in the center of Israel's camp, just as God should always be at the center of our hearts and lives.

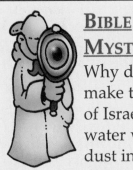

BIBLE MYSTERY

Why did Moses make the people of Israel drink water with gold dust in it?

Answer: The people had built a golden calf and worshiped it. Moses ground it into powder, put it in the water, and made the people drink it to show that they were not to have any gods except the real God.

The Ten Commandments

Here are the Ten Commandments that God gave to his people, Israel:

1. You must not have any other gods except me.
2. You must not make for yourselves any idols.
3. You must not use the name of the Lord your God thoughtlessly.
4. Remember to keep the Sabbath as a holy day.
5. Honor your father and your mother.
6. You must not murder anyone.
7. You must not be guilty of adultery.
8. You must not steal.
9. You must not tell lies about your neighbor in court.
10. You must not want to take anything that belongs to your neighbor.

Exodus 20:1–17

God said, "You must not have any other gods except me."

Exodus 20:3

God Gives Moses the Ten
Commandments

The Promised Land
Is Conquered

God Appoints Judges
to Rule Israel

1445 B.C.

1406–1400 B.C.

1380 B.C.

1400 B.C.—Anyang becomes
the capital of the Shang
dynasty.

1400 B.C.—The city of Ravenna is
founded by Italic tribes.

1400 B.C.—The Minoan-
Linear A script writing,
developed in 1900 B.C.
and in common use
since, is replaced by
Linear B script.

1380 B.C.—
Akhenaten rules
Egypt with
Nefertiti as his
queen-consort.

1406–1400 B.C. The Promised Land!

*Numbers &
Deuteronomy*

History & Politics

Egypt. Amenhotep III, a peaceful ruler, was on the throne.

*T*he Agreement with God had been made, and the people of Israel promised to keep it. The Holy Tent had been built, according to God's rules. And Abraham's family had, at last, become a strong, independent nation. God had kept his first promise to Abraham.

Now, it was time for God to keep his second promise to Abraham–that his family, Israel, would be given a special land in which to live. It was time for Israel to march into Canaan–the Promised Land–and capture it for their home. So, away they went toward Canaan.

The Grumblers

*E*ver since the people of Israel left Egypt, they had been grumbling and complaining to Moses. They complained about the food, the weather, the lack of water, the lack of meat, and all sorts of other things. They often forgot that God

58

had always protected and loved them, and that he would keep on doing so.

When they finally reached the Jordan River, they stopped to prepare for entering Canaan. Moses sent twelve spies—one from each of the twelve tribes—into Canaan to explore the land.

When they returned, ten of the spies reported that the people of Canaan were giants and that Israel couldn't defeat them. But two of the spies, Caleb and Joshua, disagreed. They said the land was rich and full of good things to eat. They believed that with God's help they could defeat Canaan and conquer the Promised Land.

When they heard the reports, the people of Israel were afraid. They forgot that God was on their side and had promised to give them the victory over their enemies in Canaan. They didn't want to attack Canaan.

Literature & Theater

A large library in the Hittite capital contained stone tablets with writings in eight different languages.

Hattusas

Religion, Philosophy & Learning

The books of Deuteronomy and Joshua in the Bible were probably written.

Visual Arts

Scandinavia. Artists began working with bronze.

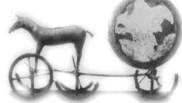

BIBLE MYSTERY
How could you tell when the men of Israel were in mourning?
Answer: They cut off their beards or pulled the hairs out with their hands. See Ezra 9:3.

Science, Technology & Growth

Mediterrania and Scandinavia. Ship building became much more advanced.

Daily Life

Egypt. Export and import trade greatly increased with countries around the world.

Israel is Punished

God became angry that his people thought they couldn't capture the Promised Land, even with his help. So he punished them by making them wander in the desert for forty long years. He said that none of them over the age of twenty, except for Joshua and Caleb, would be allowed to go into the Promised Land. They would all die in the desert. And that's exactly what happened.

Aaron and Miriam were among the ones who died. And even Moses was not allowed to go into the Promised Land because he had disobeyed God

Mind Meld

Caleb said, "We should go up and take the land for ourselves. We can do it. "

Numbers 13:30

during the time Israel wandered in the desert. God let Moses look over into Canaan from a mountain, but he could not go in.

DID YOU KNOW THAT...

no one knows where Moses was buried? When Moses died, God himself buried Moses, and only he knows where. (See Deuteronomy 34:5–7)

How Were the Pyramids Built?

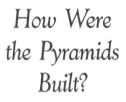

The Egyptian pyramids are one of the wonders of the world. They were made of giant cut stones, but they were built without any kind of machines. They were all built with manpower alone. One of the largest pyramids contained nearly 2,300,000 stones.

The men who built the pyramids were not slaves, as many people have thought, but they were peasant farmers. They worked for the King of Egypt and were paid for their work in food, oil, and cloth. They may have thought that helping the king get ready for his burial would please their false gods, and they would be rewarded in what they called the "next world."

The huge, hand-cut stones were often brought from stone quarries across the Nile River from where the pyramids were built. The stones were loaded onto rafts and float-

HISTORY MYSTERY

Where is the city of Aten? *Answer: Aten was about 200 miles north of Thebes, Egypt. It was built by King Amenhotep IV in honor of the false god, Aten. When Amenhotep died, the city was deserted and left to decay.*

ed across the river while it was flooded. The stone blocks weighed an average of 2,300 kilograms (5,060 pounds). From the river the blocks of stone were dragged on sledges (like sleds). Wheels were not used at all.

Then ramps made out of dirt and rubble were built beside the pyramid, and the stones were pulled up the ramps to the upper layers of the pyramids. When the pyramid was finished, the ramps were taken away. Some pyramids took about twenty years to build.

A New Leader

Joshua became leader of Israel after Moses died. Under his leadership, and with God at their side, Israel conquered Canaan and received the land God promised to their father Abraham so many years before. It was a beautiful land God had prepared especially for them. In the same way, God has prepared a special land called Heaven for us some day, if we continue to love and obey him.

The Promised Land Is Conquered	God Appoints Judges to Rule Israel	Ruth, Naomi, and Boaz
1406–1400 B.C.	1380 B.C.	1100 B.C.

1400 B.C.—The Minoan-Linear A script writing, developed in 1900 B.C. and in common use since, is replaced by Linear B script.

1380 B.C.—Akhenaten rules Egypt with Nefertiti as his queen-consort.

1361 B.C.—Tutankhamen takes the throne of Egypt when he is nine years old.

1200 B.C.—Iron smelting is perfected.

1190 B.C.—The Trojan war occurs.

1380 B.C.

Book of Judges

Here Come the Judges

Joshua led the people of Israel in victory over their enemies throughout the Promised Land of Canaan. And yet, Israel did not completely drive out their enemies. That was a big mistake. Over time, the people of Israel settled into their lands and began to farm next to their neighbors who worshiped false gods, such as Baal. And because Baal was thought to rule over farming, Israel's farmers were tempted to worship this false god, too.

From Joshua to Judges

When Joshua was 110 years old, he died. He had been a great and faithful leader of God's people, and God had blessed him greatly. After he died, Israel began to forget God once again. When the people forgot him, God allowed their enemies to defeat them. Then they would

History & Politics

1304 B.C. Egypt. Ramses II became king.

Literature & Theater

• Egypt. The people of Israel are first mentioned in an Egyptian victory hymn.

• 1380–1050 B.C. Canaan. The Book of Ruth in the Bible was probably written.

63

Religion, Philosophy & Learning

Canaan. The Age of the Judges was going on.

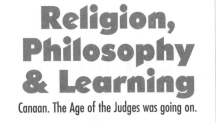

remember God and call out to him for help. And each time, God heard his people's cries and, because he loved them, would send a leader to rescue them. These leaders were called judges.

For about the next four hundred years, each time the people of Israel changed their hearts and returned to God, he would rescue them. He sent twelve judges in all, one after the other, to save Israel. Here are the names of the twelve judges, in the order they ruled Israel: Othniel, Ehud, Shamgar, Deborah, Gideon, Tola, Jair, Jephthah, Ibzan, Elon, Abdon, and Samson.

BIBLE MYSTERY

Who wore clothes that were so special they didn't wear out for forty years?
Answer: The people of Israel. God kept their clothes from wearing out while they were wandering in the desert. See Deuteronomy 29:5.

Judge Deborah

All of the judges were men, except for one–Deborah. She was a wise woman, who was respected by the people. She often sat under a huge palm tree known as the Palm of Deborah and held court there. The people of Israel came to her with their problems and complaints, and she helped them solve their problems. Deborah was a brave leader, who led Israel into battle and defeated their ene-mies. God was with her in whatever she did.

Throughout the time of the judges, Israel seemed to be on a seesaw. Some of the time they worshiped God the way he meant for them to do; other times, they forgot about God and worshiped false gods. When they worshiped God, they

Visual Arts

Mycenae. The famous Beehive Tomb was found, along with the treasury of Atreus.

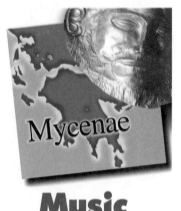

Music

China. During the Shang Dynasty, the Chinese people developed high-quality bronze casting. With this process they made the first bells.

"Then Israel cried to the Lord. So the Lord sent a man to save them."

Judges 3:9

Science, Technology & Growth

- 1300 B.C. Egypt. Scientists in Egypt identified all five planets and forty-three constellations that can be seen without a telescope.
- 1350 B.C. Syria. The process of welding was invented.

Daily Life

1350 B.C. Egypt and Greece. Showers for bathing were invented and put into use.

were happy and lived well. But when they worshiped false gods, they were unhappy and lived poorly.

In the same way, we will always be happier and live better when our hearts and lives are right with God. When we forget him, we are sad and hurting. God loves us, just as he loved Israel, and he always wants the best for us. If we pray to him when we are in trouble, he will always save us.

Have you ever noticed ...

How many times
the number twelve
comes up in the Bible?
There were:
Twelve sons of Jacob,
Twelve tribes of Israel,
Twelve spies into Canaan,
Twelve judges of Israel,
Twelve apostles of Christ, and
Twelve gates into heaven.

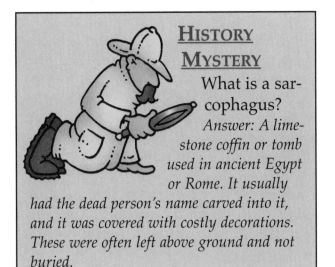

HISTORY MYSTERY

What is a sar-cophagus?

Answer: A lime-stone coffin or tomb used in ancient Egypt or Rome. It usually had the dead person's name carved into it, and it was covered with costly decorations. These were often left above ground and not buried.

Who Is Tutankhamen?

Tutankhamen (TOO-tan-kah-men) was the king of Egypt, who ruled around 1350 B.C. He followed King Amenhotep IV. He was one of the youngest kings who ruled Egypt, beginning when he was only nine years old. He ruled about ten years, and then he died at only 18 or 19.

During his reign as King of Egypt, Tutankhamen repaired many temples of the Egyptian false gods. Very little is known about his life because he died so young.

Tutankhamen was buried in the Valley of the Kings in a tomb that was so well hidden it was not found until A.D. 1922. Unlike tombs of other kings, his tomb had not been robbed. It was filled with amazing treasures and pieces of art. The treasures in the tomb explained much about ancient Egypt and showed how skilled their artists and craftsmen were.

The tomb had four rooms containing the king's personal things, such as thrones, beds, chariots, clothes, and idols of Egypt's false gods. Many of the items were made of gold, ivory, and gems. But the most wonderful treasure was King Tutankhamen's coffin. It was solid gold, and inside was a mask and headpiece made to look like the king himself. The mask was made of gold, ebony, and turquoise. It's thought to be one of the most beautiful treasures of the world today. If you're ever in Cairo, Egypt, you can see it for yourself.

God Appoints Judges to Rule Israel	Ruth, Naomi, and Boaz	Samson Is the Judge in Israel
1380 B.C.	1100 B.C.	1090 B.C.

1370 B.C.—The Sea Peoples destroy the ancient city of Ugarit.

1365 B.C.—Assyria regains its independence from Mitanni.

1304 B.C.—Ramses II becomes pharaoh of Egypt.

1100 B.C.—The sheng mouth organ is developed in China.

1085 B.C.—Egypt is split in two during the Late Dynastic Period.

1100 B.C.

A Love Story

Book of Ruth

History & Politics

1116–1077 B.C.

- Assyria. Tiglath-Pileser founded the Assyrian Empire and conquered Babylon.

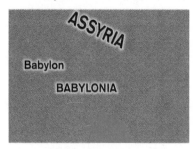

ASSYRIA

Babylon

BABYLONIA

- Mediterranean. The Phoenicians rose to power. Their cities, Tyre and Sidon, became famous for purple dye, glass, and metal goods.

During the times of the judges in Israel, there was a famine (a time when no food grows) in Israel. Elimelech, his wife, and their two sons moved to the country of Moab where there was food.

After a while, Elimelech died and left his wife, Naomi, with their two sons. When they were old enough, Naomi's two sons married women from Moab. About ten years later, both of Naomi's sons died, leaving Naomi with her two daughters-in-law, Orpah and Ruth, to care for.

Soon Naomi heard that God had once again blessed Israel with food, so Naomi, Orpah, and Ruth prepared to go back to Israel. On the way, Naomi told Orpah and Ruth to go back to their own families in Moab where they would be safe and happy. Orpah did as Naomi asked, but Ruth wouldn't leave Naomi. She promised to stay with Naomi always, to become part of her family in Israel, and to worship Naomi's God.

Ruth Meets Boaz

Ruth went to work in the grain fields in Israel to find food. She first went to the fields of Boaz, one of Naomi's close relatives. When Boaz saw Ruth, he was pleased. He had heard how good Ruth was to Naomi, even though Ruth was a Gentile (a person not from Israel). He told his servants to leave extra grain in the field for Ruth.

When a man of Israel died, it was the custom for his closest male relative to buy his land and marry his wife. Naomi thought Boaz was her closest male relative; so she sent Ruth to see him. Boaz said he wanted to buy the land and marry Ruth, but another relative was closer kin to Naomi than he was.

It's a FACT!

To seal a bargain in Israel, one man took off his sandal and gave it to the other man. In this story Naomi's close relative gave his sandal to Boaz in front of the leaders of the city. (See Ruth 4:7–12.)

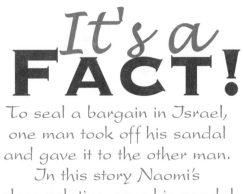

Literature & Theater

1200 B.C. Babylon. The poem, *The Just Sufferer*, showed the people becoming unhappy with their false gods.

Visual Arts

1200 B.C. Cyprus. The first enamel work was done by Mycenaeans. Enamel is a metal surface decorated with glass.

Music

China. The sheng mouth organ was developed.

Science, Technology & Growth

- China. Scientists measured the height of the sun in relation to the incline of the polar axis.

- Anatolia (Turkey). Hittites dug narrow tunnels under their city walls. During a war, they could dash out and surprise the enemy surrounding them.

Daily Life

- Egypt. Widespread robbery of the royal tombs was taking place.
- 1100 B.C. Assyria. Soldiers developed the first high-laced boot.

The Bargain

The next day Boaz found the closer relative and asked if he would buy Naomi's land and marry Ruth. The man said he couldn't do it. Then Boaz said he would buy Naomi's land and marry Ruth.

Mind Meld

Ruth said to Naomi, "Don't ask me to leave you… Every place you go, I will go. Every place you live, I will live. Your people will be my people. Your God will be my God."

Ruth 1:16

The Marriage

Soon Boaz married Ruth, and they had a baby boy named Obed. Naomi was so excited! She took the baby and helped raise him as if he were her own son. And they lived happily together as a family in Israel.

This love story is important because Obed later became the grandfather of David, King of Israel. And through David's family God's Son, Jesus, was later born into the world. It was all part of God's wonderful plan to save the people he loved.

BIBLE MYSTERY
What did it mean when Naomi took Ruth's baby onto her lap?
Answer: It meant that Naomi wanted to adopt the baby as her own child so that her husband's family name would not be lost. (See Ruth 4:14–17.)

Legend of the Trojan Horse

Two great epic poems by the famous Greek poet, Homer, are called The Iliad and The Odyssey. The first poem describes how an ancient city named Troy, on the coast of the country we call Turkey today, was attacked by a Greek army led by King Agamemnon of Mycenae. The Greek soldiers surrounded Troy for ten long years, but they could never capture it.

Finally, the Greeks won the ten-year battle by tricking the people of Troy. They built a huge wooden horse and left it just outside the gates of Troy. Then the Trojans watched as the Greek army sailed away. Sinon, a Greek spy, talked the Trojans into bringing the horse into the city. Curious about the horse, they did as Sinon had said and pulled the wooden horse inside the city.

That night Sinon opened a door in the stomach of the huge horse and let out Greek soldiers who were hidden inside. The soldiers crept out, killed the guards at the city gates, and opened the gates. The entire Greek army, who had come back secretly, came in, captured the city of Troy, and burned it down.

In the city of Troy today, there is a huge wooden horse like the one in the legend. Children can climb a ladder into its stomach and pretend to be Greek soldiers.

Ruth, Naomi and Boaz	Samson Is the Judge in Israel	Saul Is Anointed Israel's First King
1100 B.C.	1090 B.C.	1043 B.C.
1100 B.C.—The sheng mouth organ is developed in China.	1085 B.C.—Egypt is split in two during the Late Dynastic Period.	1027 B.C.—The Shang dynasty is overthrown in China and the Zhou dynasty begins.

1090–1050 B.C. *Judges 13–16* Samson: God's Strong Man

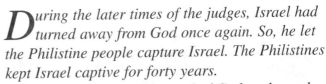

History & Politics

1090–945 B.C. Egypt. Civil war (Egyptians fighting other Egyptians) was fought while Ramses XI was King of Egypt.

*D*uring the later times of the judges, Israel had turned away from God once again. So, he let the Philistine people capture Israel. The Philistines kept Israel captive for forty years.

Then one day an angel of God spoke to the wife of Manoah, a man from Israel. The angel told Manoah's wife that she would have a baby and that the baby was to be given to God's service from the first day he was born. He was never to cut his hair. He would save Israel from the power of the Philistines.

When this baby grew up, he became one of the most interesting and exciting judges of Israel. His name was Samson, and God made him the strongest man that ever lived, even until today.

72

Samson's Secret

The secret of Samson's strength was his hair. He promised God he would never cut it. As long as he didn't cut it, he had superhuman strength from God, and he defeated thousands of Philistines. But if he ever cut his hair, he would become as weak as any other man.

Samson was strong, but he had one big weakness—he liked women too much. One woman he loved was Delilah, but she was a spy for the Philistines. Some Philistine kings offered to pay Delilah a lot of money to find out the secret to Samson's strength.

Several times Delilah asked Samson where his strength came from. Each time he told her a lie. But finally, Samson got tired of Delilah bothering him and told her his secret. Then, while he was sleeping in her lap, she cut off his hair. When he woke up, Samson was as weak as any other man.

Then the Philistines captured Samson and poked his eyes out. They took him to the city of Gaza, where they put him in bronze chains in prison. But his hair started to grow again.

Religion, Philosophy & Learning

Israel. The Age of the Judges continued.

Visual Arts

Assur. Giant tower temples were built for their false gods.

1000 B.C. China. Ice was being used. They cut ice from frozen lakes during the winter and stored it to chill food in the summer.

Daily Life

China. Prohibition (a law against drinking alcohol) was put into place.

Samson's Revenge

Sometime later the Philistine kings were having a feast for their false god Dagon. They brought Samson in to perform for them. Then they stood him between the huge pillars (posts) that held up the roof to the temple where they were. Samson put his hands out to his sides, one on each of the two huge pillars. Then he prayed that God would give him super-human strength one more time.

DID YOU KNOW THAT...

Samson told this riddle to the Philistines:
"Out of the eater comes something to eat.
Out of the strong comes something sweet."
Can you guess the answers?
See Judges 14:5–6, 8–9
Answers: A lion and honey.

Samson said, "Let me die with the Philistines!" Then, with God's help, he pushed with all his might. The pillars broke apart, and down came the temple on top of Samson and the Philistines. Samson died, but so did thousands of Philistines. God had saved his people again.

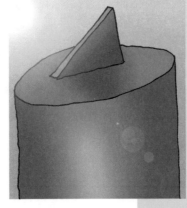

"You… will have a son. You must never cut his hair because he will be a Nazirite… He will begin the work of saving Israel from the power of the Philistines. "

Judges 13:5

Ancient Clocks

People have always wanted to know what time it is. Today we wear watches and have electric clocks. But telling time in ancient days was much harder. Here are some examples:

Sundials. 1500 B.C. Egypt. These were sometimes called "shadow clocks," because they used a shadow to tell time. The Egyptians hammered posts into the ground. The length of the shadow from the sun told the time. This was not very accurate, but it was better than nothing.

By about 700 B.C. the sundial had become much as sundials are today. The arm on the sundial (called the "gnomon") was tilted and made a shadow that stayed the same length all day. The shadow's angle, rather than its length, on the round scale told the time.

Water clocks. 1600 B.C. Egypt. The first water clocks were not much better than leaking buckets with lines up the sides. As the water dripped out, the water level went lower, and they could tell about what time it was by the lines on the bucket.

Later, an Egyptian inventor named Ctesibius of Alexandria made a more accurate water clock. It had gears and was called a "clepsydra." It measured time in Egyptian hours, which changed in length according to the season.

Sand clocks. A.D. 1300. The sandglass, sometimes called the "hourglass," was probably first used in the Middle Ages. Sand flowed through a tiny hole from a glass bulb above to a glass bulb below. When all the sand had emptied into the bottom bulb, a certain amount of time had passed. For instance, if it was an hourglass, an hour had passed.

Samson Is the Judge in Israel	Saul Is Anointed Israel's First King	David Becomes King of Israel
1090 B.C.	1043 B.C.	1004 B.C.

1085 B.C.—Egypt is split in two during the Late Dynastic Period.

1027 B.C.—The Shang dynasty is overthrown in China and the Zhou dynasty begins.

1000 B.C.—The Mound Builders are active in North America.

1043 B.C.

1 Samuel 1–15

Saul: Israel's First King

History & Politics

1000 B.C.
- North America. A people known as the Mound-builders were building burial mounds and other large works of dirt.

- India. Alexander the Great invaded the country.

*T*he last great judge in Israel was a man named Samuel. He was also a great prophet of God. The Promised Land, Canaan, was almost completely under Israel's control. And God knew the time had come when the people of Israel would reject him as their only king. They would want a human king, like the nations around them. So, he sent Samuel to anoint the king he had chosen. The kings would not rule with their own power, but with the power of God.

Saul Was Chosen

*G*od lead a young man named Saul to the city where Samuel was, and Samuel told him that God had selected him to be king over Israel. Saul was surprised because he came from the tribe of

76

Benjamin–the smallest tribe in Israel. But God had prepared Saul to be king. He was a good man, and he was a head taller than anyone else in Israel.

Saul became king when he was thirty years old, and he was King of Israel for forty-two years. He was a brave leader, but he was only a man, so he made some mistakes. His biggest mistake was that he didn't always obey God. This made God sad.

Saul's Sin

One time Samuel told Saul that God was going to punish the Amalekite people because they had ambushed the Israelites when they were leaving Egypt. God wanted Saul to attack the Amalekites and totally destroy everything that belonged to them.

So, Saul called his army together, and they attacked the City of Amalek. They destroyed everything that belonged

BIBLE MYSTERY
What do you feed an angel?
Answer: Whatever you feed people! Gideon served an angel roasted goat, bread, and soup. See Judges 6:19.

Israel. The Age of the Kings was begun.

Music

Israel. David was composing songs, which he played for King Saul. These songs and prayers set to music later became part of the Book of Psalms in the Bible.

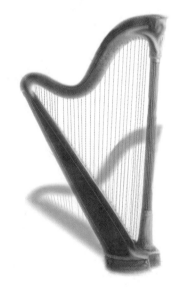

Science, Technology & Growth

1000 B.C. India. Sugarcane was being grown and made into syrup.

Daily Life

Phoenicia. Tin was being imported from mines in England.

to the Amalekites... almost. They took King Agag captive, and they kept some of the things that were good, such as the best sheep and cattle, camels and donkeys. Saul did not obey all of God's command.

Samuel met Saul and told him that God was not happy because Saul had dis-

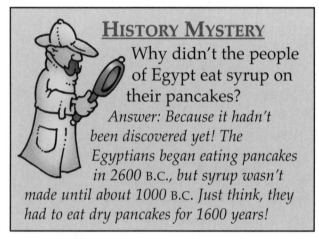

HISTORY MYSTERY

Why didn't the people of Egypt eat syrup on their pancakes?
Answer: Because it hadn't been discovered yet! The Egyptians began eating pancakes in 2600 B.C., but syrup wasn't made until about 1000 B.C. Just think, they had to eat dry pancakes for 1600 years!

Mind Meld

Israel said, "Give us a king to rule over us like all the other nations."

1 Samuel 8:5

obeyed him. Then he told Saul that God would not allow Saul's family to be kings of Israel after Saul died. Another family would be appointed as Israel's kings.

Saul's Insanity

As time went by, Saul became jealous and angry because his family would no longer be kings. When Saul's mind became upset thinking about it, a young man named David would calm Saul by playing his harp and singing for him. David and Jonathan, Saul's son, were best friends. But it was David's family that would become kings of Israel in Saul's place. So, the plot of God's story took an interesting turn.

DID YOU KNOW THAT...

King Saul asked a witch
to help him talk
to the spirit of Samuel,
who had died?
And Samuel appeared!
But the witch
didn't bring him back,
God did.
See 1 Samuel 28:1–19.

Slings Go Around and Around

One of the great stories of the Bible during Saul's reign as King of Israel is how David killed the Philistine giant, Goliath, using a sling. We usually think of David as a little boy in that story; we think the stones he used were pebbles; and we think that the sling was almost like a toy. But that's not really true.

Deadly weapons. In Saul's day, slings were deadly weapons. Soldiers in the armies used slings in warfare. And they were very accurate. Judges 20:16 says this: "Seven hundred of these trained soldiers... could sling a stone at a hair and not miss!" Wow! They were crack shots with slings.

Men, not boys. Slings were not toys for little boys to use either. They were used by men who had been trained to use them. When David fought Goliath, he was probably not a little boy, but a young man. After David later became king, the Bible says that some soldiers came to help him fight against Saul: "These were the men who helped David in battle... They could use either their right or left hands to shoot arrows or to sling rocks" (1 Chronicles 12:2).

Rocks, not pebbles. History tells us that the rocks used in these deadly slings were not little pebbles either. The rocks sometimes weighed as much as two pounds each! No wonder when David hit Goliath in the forehead with one it knocked him out. He'd been hit in the head with a two-pound rock slung at lightening speed!

Saul Is Anointed Israel's First King	David Becomes King of Israel	Solomon Builds the Temple of God
1043 B.C.	1004 B.C.	971–960 B.C.

1027 B.C.—The Shang dynasty is overthrown in China and the Zhou dynasty begins.

1000 B.C.—The Mound Builders are active in North America.

1000 B.C.—The Dorians invade the island of Rhodes.

935 B.C.— Sheshonk I becomes the first king of Egypt's 22nd dynasty.

1004 B.C. David: King, Warrior, Singer

The Book of 2 Samuel

History & Politics

Israel. King Saul died; King David began ruling.

Literature & Theater

- Israel. The earliest known Hebrew inscription dates from this time as the Gezer Calendar.
- Israel. The oldest books of the Old Testament were probably put into writing, including the Book of Judges.

*A*s Saul's kingship was ending, David was becoming a powerful and popular man in Israel. Because he defeated thousands of Israel's enemies, he became a hero. This made King Saul jealous and angry, so he tried to kill David several times. Each time he failed because God was taking care of David, whom he had chosen as the next king over his people.

After several years, Saul and Jonathan were both killed in battle. When David heard about it, he tore his clothes to show how sad he was, and he cried. All of Israel cried. Then David sang a funeral song to honor Saul and Jonathan, which is recorded in 2 Samuel 1:17–27.

David, the King

After Saul's death, God sent David to Hebron in Judah where he was appointed king. He ruled as king over Judah for seven years before he became king over all of Israel. David was thirty years old when he became king, and he ruled for forty years. He was the greatest king that Israel ever had.

Before David became king, the Jebusites had captured the city of Jerusalem, the Holy City of God. And the Ark of the Agreement of the Lord had been removed. The Ark of the Agreement was a special wooden box that held the stone tablets of the Ten Commandments.

David and his armies attacked Jerusalem and defeated the Jebusites. From that time until now, Jerusalem has been also called the City of David. Later, David and the people of Israel found the Ark of the Agreement and brought it

HISTORY MYSTERY
Where was pasta first made and eaten?

Answer: Did you say Italy? Most people would, but pasta was first made and eaten in China around the time of King David.

Religion, Philosophy & Learning

- 1000 B.C. Peru. The people of Peru began worshiping a false god that looked like a cat.

Music

Israel. The Book of Psalms, Israel's Songbook, was being written by King David, Asaph, and others.

1000 B.C. South Africa. Dogs were first used for hunting.

Daily Life

Babylon. The first sausages were created using spiced meat. Now there was sausage to go with the pancakes and syrup!

back to Jerusalem. As they came into the city, David danced before the Lord, the choirs sang, and the musicians played their flutes, lyres, harps, and trumpets to announce the Ark's arrival. It was a great day for Israel!

David, the Man

David tried hard to do everything God told him to do, but sometimes he failed. One time he stole another man's wife and had the man killed in battle. But later, he was very sad for his sin and turned back to God. And that's what made David such a great king and leader of Israel—when he made mistakes, he admitted his wrong and came back to the God who loved him.

Mind Meld

"The Lord has looked for the kind of man he wants. The Lord has appointed him (David) to become ruler of his people. "

1 Samuel 13:14

The Bible says that "David was the kind of man God wanted" (1 Samuel 13:14). He wasn't perfect, because no man can be perfect, but he tried his hardest to do what God wanted. That's why God later sent his Son Jesus into the world through David's family.

DID YOU KNOW THAT...

the Book of Psalms, which contains many songs and prayers written by King David, is the longest book in the Bible?

BIBLE MYSTERY

What was unusual about the giant that David fought at Gath?

Answer: He had twelve fingers and twelve toes! (See 2 Samuel 21:20–21.)

Israel's Songbook

The Book of Psalms in the Bible is made up of songs, poems, and prayers. It is sometimes called Israel's Songbook. Many of the songs and prayers were written by David or about David. Others were written by a man named Asaph or other men.

Besides being a great king and warrior, David was a great musician. He played the harp, wrote songs, and sang. Many of our songs about God today are the songs that David wrote when he was a shepherd for his father and a warrior in Israel.

The most famous psalm of all is Psalm 23, which was probably written when David was a shepherd. Sometimes we sing this song today.

The Lord is my shepherd.
  I have everything I need.
He gives me rest in green pastures.
  He leads me to calm water.
  He gives me new strength.
For the good of his name,
  he leads me on paths that are right.
Even if I walk
  through a very dark valley,
I will not be afraid
  because you are with me.
Your rod and your walking stick
  comfort me.

You prepare a meal for me
  in front of my enemies.
You pour oil on my head.
  You give me more than I can hold.
Surely your goodness and
  love will be with me all my life.
And I will live in the house of the Lord
  forever.
(International Children's Bible)

1000 B.C.—The Mound Builders are active in North America.

1000 B.C.—The Gezer, the earliest known Hebrew inscription, is dated to this period.

935 B.C.—Sheshonk I becomes the first king of Egypt's 22nd dynasty.

971–960 B.C.

Solomon: The Wisest Man

History & Politics

Israel. The Temple to Yahweh (God) was built by Solomon in Jerusalem, and Israel reached the height of its civilization.

Literature & Theater

Israel. The Bible books of Proverbs, Song of Songs, and Ecclesiastes were probably written.

1 Kings 1–11

*W*hen David, the "sweet singer of Israel," died, he was buried in the City of David. Right after that, his son Adonijah tried to make himself king. But that was not God's plan, and David's son Solomon was appointed king instead. Right away, Solomon had Adonijah killed. Then Solomon married the daughter of the King of Egypt, in order to stop Egypt from becoming Israel's enemy again. Then Solomon's first few years as King of Israel were peaceful and calm.

Solomon's Wisdom

One night God spoke to King Solomon in a dream. God said, "Ask for anything you want. I will give it to you." And Solomon said, "I ask that you give me wisdom. Then I can rule the people in the right way." God was pleased with Solomon's answer. So he made Solomon the wisest man who ever lived, both then and now. He also gave Solomon great riches and honor. During his time, there was no other king as great as Solomon.

Visual Arts
China. Brush-and-ink paintings were done.

Music
Israel. Professional musicians performed at religious ceremonies.

Solomon's Temple

King David had wanted to build a great temple for God in Jerusalem, but God did not allow David to build it. So, about four years after Solomon became king, he took the plans his father had drawn and built the temple just as the Lord wanted it.

This amazing temple was the most beautiful temple ever built. And it took over seven years to build it. The temple meant that God was still living among his people, just as he had lived in the Holy Tent when they were traveling in the desert after they left Egypt.

Science, Technology & Growth

Mediterranean. Fabric dyes were made from purple snails.

Daily Life

Egypt and Assyria. Wigs were worn by wealthy people.

Solomon's Fame

Just as he had promised, God gave Solomon great wisdom, amazing riches, and the highest honor possible. His kingdom was the most peaceful and wealthy that had ever been known. He was so famous that the Queen of Sheba traveled over 1,200 miles by camel through the desert to see if what she had heard about King Solomon was really true. After she saw Solomon and his kingdom, she said, "I was not told even half of it! Your wisdom and wealth are much greater than I had heard."

"I ask that you give me wisdom. Then I can rule the people in the right way… Without wisdom, it is impossible to rule this great people of yours."

1 Kings 3:9

What Are Proverbs?

King Solomon wrote thousands of wise sayings or "proverbs." These proverbs were often written as short, two-line poems called "couplets." They gave good advice on the right way for people to live and act.

Some proverbs show the difference between good and evil:
"People who do what is right will have rich blessings. But the wicked will be overwhelmed by violence" (Proverbs 10:6).

Some proverbs show the difference between wise people and foolish people:
"A lazy person will end up poor.
But a hard worker will become rich" (Proverbs 10:4).

Other proverbs show the difference in what is honest and what is dishonest:
"An honest witness tells the truth.
But a dishonest witness tells lies" (Proverbs 12:17).

And some proverbs point out the good habits of some of God's creatures:
"Ants are not very strong.
But they store up food in the summer" (Proverbs 30:25).

In all, Solomon and some other wise people recorded over 600 wise sayings. You can read these in your Bible in the Book of Proverbs.

Solomon's Writings

Because Solomon was so wise, he wrote wise sayings and songs to teach the people about God and life. The wise sayings are called "proverbs." The Bible books of Proverbs, Ecclesiastes, and Song of Songs, as well as some of the Psalms, are all thought to be written by Solomon.

DID YOU KNOW THAT...

Solomon had over 700 wives?
He married them
to keep peace
with the nations
around Israel.

1000 B.C.—The Dorians invade the island of Rhodes.

935 B.C.—Sheshonk I becomes the first king of Egypt's 22nd dynasty.

900 B.C.—The Olmec seat of power shifts from San Lorenzo to La Venta in Mesoamerica.

900 B.C.—The Andean culture of Paracas begins to flourish.

931 B.C.
1 Kings 12–22 & 2 Chronicles

Divided!

*N*ear the end of King Solomon's reign, he thought back over the his life. He had lived with great riches, honor from other nations, a powerful kingdom, and worldwide fame–everything most people want. But those things were not worth anything to him compared to living with God forever. His final writings are called Ecclesiastes, and you can read them in your Bible.

The Kingdom Divides

When Solomon died, his son Rehoboam became king. But Israel was not happy with him as their king because he was mean and unfair to them. He was not wise as his father Solomon had been. So, ten of the twelve tribes of Israel refused to follow Rehoboam, and they chose a new king named Jeroboam. These ten tribes continued to be known as "Israel." But Jeroboam quickly led them to worship false gods, and they turned away from

History & Politics

- 931 B.C. Israel. The nation of Israel divided into Israel and Judah.
- 922 B.C. Civil war began between Israel and Judah.

Literature & Theater

- Israel. The Song of Deborah was written.
- 930 B.C. Israel. The Bible books of 1 Samuel and 2 Samuel were probably written.

Religion, Philosophy & Learning

Egypt conquered Jerusalem—the Holy City.

MEDITERRANEAN SEA

JERUSALEM

EGYPT

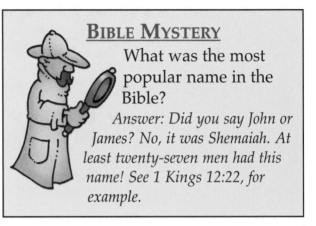

BIBLE MYSTERY

What was the most popular name in the Bible?

Answer: Did you say John or James? No, it was Shemaiah. At least twenty-seven men had this name! See 1 Kings 12:22, for example.

Visual Arts

• Greece. Geometric designs were being used on Greek works of art.

• Northern Europe. Gold vessels and jewelry were being made and used.

the God who had always loved them and saved them from their enemies.

The other two tribes, Judah and Benjamin, stayed with Rehoboam as their king and became known as "Judah." It was this smaller group of Hebrew people who remained faithful to God most of the time. Because of this, the Levites (those appointed as priests for the Hebrew people) and other good people in Israel who wanted to follow God moved south to join with Judah.

The Two Kingdoms

For the next 100 years, Judah had good kings, like Asa and his son Jehoshaphat, who followed God's law and kept the people faithful to him. Here's what the Bible says about Asa: "Asa did what the Lord said was good and right. He removed the foreign altars used for idol worship. He removed the places where false gods were worshiped. He smashed the stone pillars that honored false gods... Asa commanded the people of Judah to obey... the Lord's teachings and commandments" (2 Chronicles 14:2–4).

But Israel had seven evil kings in a row, who led them to worship false gods. So, the two kingdoms of God's people fought with each other and the nations around them.

The kingdom of God was divided, and it would never be united again, until Jesus was born hundreds of years later. It was a very sad time for God's people.

"Since then, Israel has always turned against the family of David (Judah)."

2 Chronicles 10:19

Science, Technology & Growth

- Greece. Iron was first used.

- Israel. Underground water tunnels were built in Jerusalem.

Daily Life

Israel. The flowing caftan (a long, loose robe) was first worn by the Hebrew women.

The Art of Writing

From earliest times, people have written things down for others to read. And through the centuries, the tools for writing, such as pens and inks, have changed.

Mesopotamia. The first writing that we know about was on clay tablets in Mesopotamia. Writers (called "scribes") used a wedge-shaped pen to make marks in the clay while it was still wet. When the clay dried, it left a record that could not be changed. This was called "cuneiform" writing.

Egypt and Assyria. Scribes in ancient Egypt and Assyria wrote on papyrus. This was made from pith taken from the stem of the papyrus plant. The pith was removed, put into layers, and hammered together to make a smooth surface for writing. Scribes wrote with reeds and rushes, which had been whittled to a writing point. Their ink was made from lampblack—soot from the oil they burned in lamps, mixed with water and plant gums.

China. The people of early China wrote their characters in ink using brushes made of camels' or rats' hairs. Groups of hairs were glued and bound to the end of a stick and dipped in ink. All 10,000 or more Chinese writing characters are based on just eight brush strokes.

Today. We have many choices of writing tools today, which have been developed from these ancient ones—pencils, ball-point pens, fountain pens, felt-tip pens, and others. And we have many different colors of ink. In the early days, writing was hard work, but today it's fun.

It's a FACT!

The Bible says "Do not be afraid" 365 times—that's once for every day of the year. We should never be afraid with God on our side. Israel forgot that.
See Luke 1:30

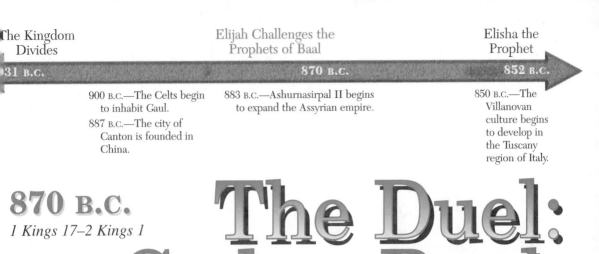

The Kingdom
Divides

Elijah Challenges the
Prophets of Baal

Elisha the
Prophet

31 B.C.

870 B.C.

852 B.C.

900 B.C.—The Celts begin
to inhabit Gaul.
887 B.C.—The city of
Canton is founded in
China.

883 B.C.—Ashurnasirpal II begins
to expand the Assyrian empire.

850 B.C.—The
Villanovan
culture begins
to develop in
the Tuscany
region of Italy.

870 B.C.
1 Kings 17–2 Kings 1

The Duel: God vs. Baal

*D*uring the years that God's people were divided
into the two kingdoms of Israel and Judah, God
kept on loving them. Even though they didn't love
and obey him, he kept on loving them. When the two
kingdoms were not following him, God knew they
were like lost children who didn't know which way to
go. So, he sent great men of faith to show them the
way back to him. The men were called prophets. They
brought messages from God to his people.

Elijah's Message

*O*ne of the greatest of all prohets to
Israel was Elijah. God sent him to
speak out against King Ahab and his wife,
Jezebel. Elijah told them that, because of
their evil ways in worshiping the false god
Baal, it would not rain again until he said
it would. Right away, the rain stopped,
and it didn't rain again in Israel for three
years!

History & Politics

- Israel. The city of Samaria was rebuilt
  as capital of Israel, the northern kingdom.

- Cyprus. The people of Phoenicia settled
  on the island.

- 870 B.C. Israel. King Ahab married the
  princess of Phoenicia, Jezebel. They
  were two of the most evil people ever
  to live.

93

Literature & Theater

Greece. Homer wrote the two long, epic poems called Iliad and Odyssey.

Religion, Philosophy & Learning

Israel. The Age of the Prophets began.

Visual Arts

Assyria. The royal palace and temple to the false god Ishtar were rebuilt in the city of Nineveh.

Finally, God sent Elijah back to Ahab. He told Ahab to bring all the people of Israel, the 450 prophets of Baal, and the 400 prophets of Asherah (another false god), to Mount Carmel to meet him.

The Duel

On the mountain Elijah challenged Israel and the prophets of Baal to a duel. He said, "If the Lord is the true God, follow him. But if Baal is the true God, follow him" (1 Kings 18:21)! He said the prophets of Baal would prepare one sacrifice, and he would prepare another. Then they would call on Baal, and he would call on God. Whichever god answered the prayers

DID YOU KNOW THAT...

while Elijah was hiding from King Ahab, God sent ravens to feed him with bread and meat every day?
See 1 Kings 17:1–6.

and burned up the sacrifice would be the true God. And the people agreed that it was a good plan.

The prophets of Baal went first. They called on their false god from morning until night. They danced around their altar, and they even cut themselves with swords to show how sincere they were. But Baal did not answer. Nothing happened.

Then it was Elijah's turn. He prepared the sacrifice as God commanded. To prove his point, he had twelve huge stone jars of water poured over the sacrifice. Then Elijah prayed to God to rain down fire from heaven to show the people that he was the one and only true God.

Suddenly, fire from heaven fell on the altar. It burned up the sacrifice. It burned up the altar. And it even licked

Science, Technology & Growth

Iron and steel was produced in Indo-Caucasian cultures. Iron saws were first made and used.

Daily Life

Assyria. The favorite royal sport was hunting from chariots. Nimrod, famous ruler of Assyria, was well known for this type of hunting.

"The LORD is God!
The LORD is God!"

1 Kings 18:39

Who Was Baal?

The word Baal meant "lord." In Elijah's time, the people of Canaan and Phoenicia worshiped a false god (idol) they called Baal. He was also called the Son of Dagon or the Son of El. In Syria he was called Hadad, and in Babylonia, he was known as Adad.

Baal was believed to be able to help women have babies. He was also thought to be the god of rain. So, when Elijah told Ahab and Jezebel that God would stop the rain, it was a direct challenge to Baal. And for three years, Baal could not make it rain.

Baal was often pictured standing on top of a bull, which was a symbol of strength. So, when fire from heaven burned up the bull on the altar on Mount Carmel, it showed that God was much stronger than Baal.

The way people worshiped Baal was wrong and evil. Sometimes they even killed their children and offered them as sacrifices to the false god. Sometimes they had sexual relations with people who were not their husbands or wives as worship to Baal. Our real God hated those evil actions.

People who worshiped Baal believed that the storm clouds were Baal's chariot. They thought that thunder was the voice of Baal speaking to them. And they believed that lightning was Baal's spear and arrows. But these were all false beliefs.

As Elijah showed with the duel on Mount Carmel, there is only one true God, and he is the Lord of heaven and earth.

up the water. Then the people of Israel fell down on the ground and bowed face-down before the Lord. They shouted, "The Lord—he is God!"

Then Elijah had all the false prophets killed. God had won the duel! Elijah did many other amazing works, too, with the Lord's help. Many of his mighty works were like the miracles Jesus did so many years later.

BIBLE MYSTERY

What prophet of God could run faster than a speeding horse?
Answer: Elijah. He outran King Ahab's chariot from Mount Carmel all the way to the city of Jezreel. See 1 Kings 18:46.

Elijah and the
Prophets of Baal

Elisha the
Prophet

Jonah and the
Big Fish

870 B.C.

852 B.C.

775 B.C.

883 B.C.—Ashurnasirpal
II begins to expand the
Assyrian empire.

850 B.C.—The Villanovan
culture begins to
develop in the Tuscany
region of Italy.

814 B.C.—The
Phoenicians found
the city of
Carthage about
this time.

776 B.C.—The
first Olym-
pic Games
are held in
Greece.

A Whirlwind and a Special Coat

852 B.C.

2 Kings 2–13

*D*uring the time that Elijah was a messenger for God, a young man named Elisha was his helper. Elisha followed Elijah around the country, watching him, talking to him, and learning how to be a prophet himself. Finally, it came time for God to take Elijah out of the world, and Elisha was going to become God's prophet in Elijah's place.

On that special day, Elijah and Elisha were traveling together. They both knew that God was going to take Elijah to heaven that day. They traveled through several towns; then they went to the Jordan River. Elijah took off his coat, rolled it up, and struck the water in the river. Then the river parted, and Elijah and Elisha walked through the river on dry ground to the other side.

Elijah said to Elisha, "What can I do for you before I am taken from you?"

Elisha said, "Leave me a double share of your spirit." He was asking for Elijah's power as a prophet to become his own.

History & Politics

- 842 B.C. Israel. Jehu takes the kingship away from Ahab's family.
- Corinth. The Dorian people conquer the city of Corinth.

97

Literature & Theater

Leather scrolls replaced clay tablets for writing purposes.

Religion, Philosophy & Learning

Eastern Mediterranean. Most countries in this region were worshiping false gods such as winged animals or the sun.

Visual Arts

Balawat. Highly developed metal and stone sculptures were being made.

Elijah said, "You have asked a hard thing. But if you see me when I am taken from you, it will be yours. If you don't, it won't happen."

The Whirlwind

As they walked on, suddenly a chariot and horses made of fire appeared. It came between Elijah and Elisha. Then Elijah was taken up to heaven by God in a whirlwind. And Elisha saw it happen. That was the last time Elisha saw Elijah; so Elisha tore his clothes to show how sad he was.

The Special Coat

Elisha picked up Elijah's coat that had fallen from him and went back to the Jordan River. He rolled up the coat and hit the water with Elijah's coat, and the river parted just as it had for Elijah. Then Elisha walked through the river on dry ground again.

A group of prophets from Jericho were watching. They said, "Elisha now has the spirit Elijah had." And they bowed down before him.

Elisha, the Prophet

Like his teacher, Elijah, Elisha did many mighty works and miracles while he served God as a messenger to Israel. And, like Elijah, Elisha's miracles were very much like the miracles that Jesus would do when he came years later.

BIBLE MYSTERY
Who was Marduk?
Answer: Marduk was a false god worshiped by the people of Babylon about 850 B.C.

Elisha said to Elijah, "Leave me a double share of your spirit."

2 Kings 2:9

China. Their history was first recorded in date order.

Daily Life

- Carthage and Tyre began trading with each other.
- Greece, Persia, Rome. Cock fighting was practiced. This sport is still popular today in Asia and Latin America.

What Were the Dark Ages?

The years from 1100 to 700 B.C. in Greece are called the Dark Ages. Why? Because so little is known about what happened during those years.

During these centuries, stories of the great Mycenaean civilization that had gone before were handed down from one generation to the next, not in writing, but in the form of poems. Two of them have been saved for us. They were written by the great poet, Homer.

Iliad. This epic poem described how the city of Troy, which is located in modern-day Turkey, was held captive by a Greek army for over ten years. The army was led by King Agamemnon of Mycenae. The poem describes the heroic deeds of Greek and Trojan soldiers like Achilles and Hektor. And it tells the wonderful story of the Trojan Horse, mentioned earlier in this book.

Odyssey. The sec-
ond epic poem by
Homer tells
the story of
one Greek
hero named
Odysseus on his
way home from
the Trojan War. It
took him ten years,
and he had many

exciting adventures as he traveled home. The poem tells about real events that happened, such as wars, battles, and captivities.

Because little history of these years was recorded in writing, they will always remain the Dark Ages.

It's a
FACT!

The iron head of an ax once floated on water. God helped Elisha
make it float.
See 2 Kings 6:1–7.

BIBLE MYSTERY

Why is it unwise to tease a baldheaded man?

Answer: Because it could be a scary experience like the boys had who teased the prophet Elisha. See what happened in 2 Kings 2:23–24.

Elisha the Prophet	Jonah and the Big Fish	Isaiah the Prophet
852 B.C.	775 B.C.	740 B.C.

850 B.C.—The Villanovan culture begins to develop in the Tuscany region of Italy.

800 B.C.—The Greek city of Corinth is founded.

776 B.C.—The first Olympic Games are held in Greece.

753 B.C.—Romulus and Remus found the city of Rome.

745 B.C.—King Tiglath-Pileser III begins the restoration of Assyrian imperial power.

A Big Fish Story

The Book of Jonah
775 B.C.

During the next sixty years after Elisha's death, the kingdoms of Israel and Judah continued to ignore God and worship idols. And God, who still loved them, sent more of his prophets to warn them to come back to him. He sent Jonah, Hosea, Joel, and Amos to different places with messages for the people. The story of Jonah is one of the most amazing ones.

God Sent Jonah

One day God told Jonah to go to the huge city of Nineveh to preach against it. Nineveh was the capital city of the Assyrian people, who didn't worship God. The kings of Assyria lived there, and it was an evil city.

Jonah didn't want to go to Nineveh, so he ran away from God. He went down to Joppa and got on a ship going to

History & Politics

Spain. The Greek people began to settle in parts of Spain.

Literature & Theater

- Egypt. A famous fable was written called *The Battle Between Head and Belly*.
- Israel. The Bible books of Jonah, Amos, and Joel were probably written.

Religion, Philosophy & Learning

Greece. The false god Apollo was worshiped at Delphi.

Visual Arts

Asia Minor. Arts and crafts were popular, including metal sculpture, carpet weaving, embroidery, and rock carving.

Tarshish. But God made a great wind blow on the sea, and the waves became very high. The ship was about to break apart! And the sailors were afraid. They started throwing things off the ship to make it lighter so it wouldn't sink. But they were still in danger.

Then the sailors threw lots (something like rolling dice) to see who had caused the storm. The lots showed that it was Jonah's fault. So Jonah told them what he had done. The men tried hard to row the ship to shore, but the storm got stronger and stronger. Finally, they did as Jonah told them—they threw Jonah into the sea.

The Big Fish

Then God caused a very big fish to swallow Jonah. He was in the stomach of the fish for three days and three nights. And

HISTORY MYSTERY
How big was the city of Nineveh?
Answer: It had over 120,000 people! And it took a person three full days just to walk around it.

while he was there, Jonah prayed to God to save him. After that, God made the fish spit Jonah out onto the shore. Then he told Jonah again to go to Nineveh and preach against it. This time, Jonah did what God said. He went to Nineveh.

When the people of Nineveh heard the message Jonah brought to them from God, they believed him. They stopped eating and wore rough cloth called "sackcloth" to show how sad they were for their sins. Everyone in the city did this—poor people, rich people, and even the king.

When God saw that all the people of Nineveh stopped doing evil things and believed in him, he changed his mind and did not punish them. God is always

Jonah said, "I am a Hebrew. I fear the Lord, the God of heaven. He is the God who made the sea and the land."

Jonah 1:9

Music

Babylonia. Both the five-tone and the seven-tone musical scales were in use.

Science, Technology & Growth

- Highly developed medical surgery was being used on the battlefields.
- The Etruscans were using hand cranks.

Daily Life

776 B.C. Greece. The first Olympic Games were held in the city of Olympia.

A Modern-Day Jonah

Could Jonah have actually been swallowed by a giant fish and lived to tell about it? Is it possible?

Yes! The average sperm whale, for instance, has a mouth twenty feet long, fifteen feet high, and nine feet wide. That's larger than most rooms in the average house. So there was plenty of room for Jonah.

In 1891 a whaling ship called the Star of the East saw a large sperm whale near the Falkland Islands. While harpooning the whale, one of the sailors named James Bartley, was lost at sea and thought to be dead.

The whale was killed and pulled to the side of the ship. Then the sailors began to remove the blubber. The next day, the whale was pulled up onto the deck of the ship. When its stomach was opened, there was James Bartley. To the surprise of everyone on the ship, he was alive! They revived him, and he lived to tell about his Jonah-like experience.

However, James had some lasting reminders of his time in the whale's stomach. The gastric juices of the whale had bleached his skin pure white. All the hair on his body was gone. And his eyes were a light blue color.

Perhaps, Jonah's skin was bleached pure white; maybe he became bald and hairless, and had piercing blue eyes, too. Could his freaky looks have been one of the reasons the people of Nineveh listened to his message and believed him?

happy when his people come back to him.

Later, when Jesus came, the Bible compared Jesus' being in the grave for three days to Jonah's being inside the great fish for three days. So the story of Jonah was a clue about what would happen some day.

Archaeologists have now found the royal library of King Ashurbanipal, who lived in Nineveh. The library contained over 25,000 clay tablets of writing!

BIBLE MYSTERY

Which Bible prophet was "for the birds"?

Answer: Jonah. His name means "dove."

776 B.C.—The first Olympic Games are held in Greece.

753 B.C.—Romulus and Remus found the city of Rome.

750 B.C.—The earliest Greek colony in Italy is founded at Cumae.

734 B.C.—Corinthians settle the island of Corfu.

722 B.C.— Peking (Beijing) becomes the capital of the Yen Kingdom in China.

740 B.C.

Isaiah: The Jesus Prophet

Isaiah 1–17

*J*onah was a prophet of God while Jeroboam II was King of Israel. During that same time, Uzziah was King of Judah. While Jonah, Amos, Hosea, and Joel took messages to Israel and Assyria, a prophet named Isaiah was God's messenger to Judah. Isaiah may have been the most powerful of all of God's prophets, and he spoke for God for forty years.

History & Politics

753 B.C. Italy. The city of Rome was founded by Romulus and Remus.

The Jesus Prophet

I saiah's message from God was that the people of Judah should repent of their terrible sins before it was too late. He warned them that they would soon be taken captive by Assyria because they continued to sin against God by worshiping false gods. Isaiah described the "terrible day of the Lord" when all the people

Religion, Philosophy & Learning

Israel & Judah. Prophets Amos, Hosea, Joel, and Isaiah fought religious and social abuses.

Literature & Theater

Israel. Collecting of The Sayings of Solomon was begun.

on earth would be judged guilty by God, just as Israel and Judah were being judged by God.

At the same time, Isaiah often talked with excitement about "the coming Messiah." Messiah means "savior." So, Isaiah was telling Judah about the coming of Jesus, the Savior who would save the people of Judah and Israel from their sins. That's why Isaiah is sometimes called "the Messianic prophet."

Some of God's messages through Isaiah tell what will happen in the future. Even though it was 700 years before Jesus would be born, Isaiah told the people of Judah that Jesus would be called "Immanuel" when he was born. He also told them that the Messiah (Jesus) would be a descendant of King David and that he would set up a kingdom of the few Hebrew people who still loved and

HISTORY MYSTERY
What kind of clothes did the athletes wear in the first Olympic Games in Greece?
Answer: None! They competed naked. That's why married women were not allowed to attend the games.

obeyed God. He said that when Jesus came, he would bring peace, justice, and joy.

God's Message to the Nations

Although the people of Judah were not faithful to God, he still loved them, and he knew they were part of his ongoing plan to bring Jesus into the world. Because Judah sinned against him, God allowed other nations to take them captive as punishment for their sins. And yet, God would also punish those nations someday for acting against Judah, the people he loved. So, God sent Isaiah to deliver messages of warning to those nations, too.

Visual Arts

Egypt, Phoenicia, Samaria. Ivory carving practiced.

Music

Mesopotamia. A system of musical notation was developed, and the earliest hymn was written down.

"He willingly gave his life. He was treated like a criminal. But he carried away the sins of many people. And he asked forgiveness for those who sinned."

Isaiah 53:12

Science, Technology & Learning

India. Medical training was done using actual models of the human body.

Daily Life

- Assyria. Men and women's clothes were almost the same.
- Bullfighting was a popular sport. It's still popular in some countries today, such as Spain and Mexico.

Hope from Hezekiah

At long last, a new king began to rule Judah. His name was Hezekiah, and he loved the Lord. During his reign, Hezekiah repaired the temple of God and

DID YOU KNOW THAT...

the name Immanuel means "God with us"? Just as God lived among the Hebrews in the Holy Tent and then in the Temple, he was planning to live among his people as Jesus someday.

returned Judah's worship to him. He even sent an invitation to the kingdom of Israel to join Judah for the annual Passover Feast. And he made many other changes to return Judah to God.

Still, God had shown Isaiah that Judah would not remain faithful to him. So Isaiah warned the people of Judah to keep doing what was right and not to go back to their sinful ways again. If they did, God said they would be taken captive by their enemies, the Assyrians.

BIBLE MYSTERY
What does it mean when the Bible says that a little child leads wild beasts around?
Answer: It means there will be peace. See Isaiah 11:6.

The Olympic Games

Our modern Olympic Games were copied from a religious festival in Greece that began during the days of the prophets. It was held in the town of Olympia in honor of the false god Zeus.

The festival lasted five days and included sports, music, and drama. Just like today, the festival was held once every four years. The athletes had to be free Greek citizens, not slaves. And they swore an oath to keep the rules.

When it was time for the Olympic Games, all wars stopped so that people from all over Greece could travel safely to the games in Olympia. At the end of the games, oxen were sacrificed to Zeus, and everyone joined in a great feast.

The main event in the first Olympic Games was the pentathlon. This event had five different sports that the athletes had to compete in—a foot race, discus throwing, wrestling, javelin throwing, and the long jump. All of these events still exist today. Those first games also included running, chariot races, horse races, and boxing matches. Today we have other events, such as gymnastics and pole vaulting.

In today's opening ceremony, an athlete lights the Olympic flame just as an athlete did in 776 B.C. Then an athlete lit the fire on the altar where a sacrifice to Zeus was made.

734 B.C.—Corinthians settle the island of Corfu.

722 B.C.—Peking (Beijing) becomes the capital of the Yen Kingdom in China.

721 B.C.—Sargon II founds the last Assyrian dynasty.

716 B.C.—Rulers of Cush conquer Egypt.

723–721 B.C.

Isaiah 18—38

Captured!

History & Politics

- 732 B.C. Israel. The Assyrian king, Tiglath-Pileser III captured the city of Damascus and made Israel a servant state.
- Babylon. The Assyrians seized the throne of Babylon.
- China. Peking became the capital of the Yen Kingdom.

"*Change your hearts and lives. Return to God, or you will be taken captive by Assyria!*" That's what God's prophets had been telling the northern tribes of Israel. But the people of Israel didn't listen, and before long they were taken captive by the Assyrians. Their homes and lands were soon stolen by people from Babylonia and other countries to the east.

Meanwhile, the two tribes of Judah were still standing against Assyria, but probably not for long. So Judah began to ask their neighbor nations for help. One of the nations they turned to was their old enemy, Egypt, with their armies of horses and chariots.

The Naked Truth

Isaiah then spoke God's message against Egypt and Cush. He was upset because Judah was depending on horses and chariots for help, rather than the power of God. So that people would notice him and listen to God's message, Isaiah—because God said to—went around naked for three years. (The word "naked" in the Hebrew language may have meant that he only took off his outside clothes. But even that was terrible!)

Live Long and Prosper

When it came time for good King Hezekiah of Judah to die, God sent Isaiah to tell him. Isaiah said, "This is what the Lord says: You are going to die. So you should give your last orders to everyone. You will not get well."

"The Lord will hear your crying, and he will comfort you. The Lord will hear you, and he will help you."

Isaiah 30:19

Music

Greece. Choral and dramatic music developed.

Science, Technology & Growth

- Babylonia, China. Astronomers first understood how planets move in their orbits.
- September 6, 775 B.C. China. A solar eclipse was recorded for the first time in Chinese history.

When he heard this, Hezekiah turned his face toward the wall and prayed that God would let him live a while longer. Then he cried loudly.

Before Isaiah left Hezekiah's palace, God told him to go back and speak to Hezekiah again. So Isaiah went back and said, "This is what the Lord said: I have heard your prayer. And I have seen your tears. So I will heal you. Three days from now you will go up to the Temple of the Lord. I will add fifteen years to your life. I will save you and this city from the king of Assyria."

HISTORY MYSTERY

What happened to Assyria's army? Why didn't they capture the city of Jerusalem? *Answer: God kept his promise to Hezekiah to defend Judah against evil Assyria. A Greek history writer named Herodotus said that field mice swarmed into the Assyrian camp. And they ate bow strings and shield handles. Some historians think that a terrible disease like the Black Plague, carried by rats and mice, killed the Assyrian soldiers. The Bible just says that God destroyed 185,000 of them.*

To show Hezekiah that what he had said was true, and that Hezekiah would live another fifteen years, God made the shadow on the stairs go backward ten steps. That's how Hezekiah knew that God could make time go backward in his own life, too. God is awesome—he can do anything!

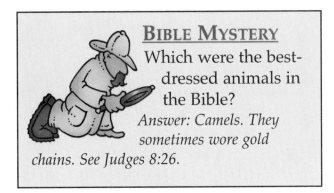

BIBLE MYSTERY
Which were the best-dressed animals in the Bible?
Answer: Camels. They sometimes wore gold chains. See Judges 8:26.

Life in Assyria

In early times, Assyria was a small, unimportant state in northern Mesopotamia. For hundreds of years, Assyria was ruled by bigger, more powerful nations like Babylon. But when these nations lost their power, Assyria became strong and built an empire of its own.

The Assyrians believed that their land belonged to Ashur, their false god. As Ashur's primary servant, the King of Assyria ruled the people. He also fought wars for Ashur and built temples to honor him. The king appointed Ashur's priests and led special religious festivals.

The King of Assyria usually had several wives and lots of children, which was against the teachings of God. When the king chose one of his sons to become king after he died, that son was sent to a special school called the House of the Succession. There he was taught how to be a good king.

One of the most famous kings of Assyria was named Ashurbanipal. This king's favorite sport was hunting. He liked to show off his skill and bravery. Sometimes lions were brought to the king's hunting parks. They were kept in cages until the king was ready to hunt them. A line of soldiers with full-body shields formed a wall to keep the lions from escaping. The Assyrian people were allowed to watch the king hunt and kill the lions. It gave them great faith in his strength and power as king.

The Assyrians grew many different foods, such as wheat, barley, grapes, fruit trees, and vegetables. And they dug deep wells inside their cities so they would always have water, even if an enemy army surrounded them.

It's a FACT!

The Assyrian people laughed at King Hezekiah for depending on God. But guess who later got the last laugh!

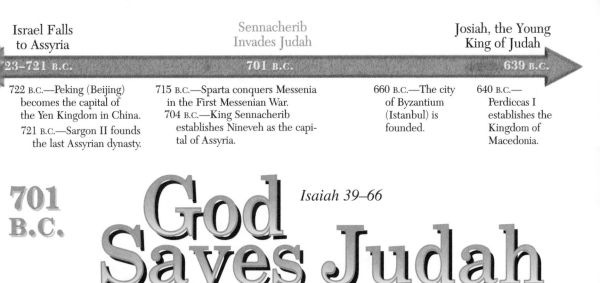

Israel Falls to Assyria	Sennacherib Invades Judah	Josiah, the Young King of Judah
23–721 B.C.	701 B.C.	639 B.C.

722 B.C.—Peking (Beijing) becomes the capital of the Yen Kingdom in China.

721 B.C.—Sargon II founds the last Assyrian dynasty.

715 B.C.—Sparta conquers Messenia in the First Messenian War.

704 B.C.—King Sennacherib establishes Nineveh as the capital of Assyria.

660 B.C.—The city of Byzantium (Istanbul) is founded.

640 B.C.— Perdiccas I establishes the Kingdom of Macedonia.

701 B.C.

God Saves Judah Again

Isaiah 39–66

*B*efore King Hezekiah of Judah almost died, Assyria had conquered most of the strong, walled cities of Judah. So Hezekiah sent a message to the King of Assyria whose name was Sennacherib. He asked Sennacherib to leave Judah alone, and he would pay Sennacherib any amount of money he wanted. Sennacherib demanded about 22,000 pounds of silver and 2,000 pounds of gold! But Hezekiah paid Sennacherib what he had asked. Then Sennacherib left… but not for long.

Here They Came Again

*S*oon Sennacherib's armies attacked Judah's strong, walled cities again, thinking they would capture them for themselves. When Hezekiah heard that

History & Politics

- 681 B.C. Assyria. King Sennacherib was murdered by two of his three sons in Nineveh. His third son, Essarhaddon, became king in his place.
- 660 B.C. Turkey. The city of Istanbul was founded. Then it was called Byzantium.
- 660 B.C. Japan. According to legend, the country of Japan was founded by Jimmu.

115

Literature & Theater

- Greece. Kallinos, the earliest known Greek lyricist lived. A lyricist writes the words to songs.
- Judah. The Book of Isaiah in the Bible was written.

Religion, Philosophy & Learning

Greece. The false gods Apollo and Dionysus became more popular.

Visual Arts

- Babylonia. King Essarhaddon rebuilt the city of Babylon.
- 700 B.C. Europe. Artists began working with iron instead of bronze.

Assyria was attacking them again, he worked hard to protect the city of Jerusalem. He and the people repaired the city walls and built another wall around the outside of that. He had towers built on the walls, and he gathered his armies together ready to fight.

Then Hezekiah went to the Temple and prayed to God: "Lord our God, save us from the king's power. Then all the kingdoms of the earth will know that you, Lord, are the only God." Later Isaiah came and told Hezekiah that God had heard his prayer, and that he would save Jerusalem from Assyria, just as he had promised before.

That night 185,000 of Sennacherib's soldiers died. When the Assyrian people got up the next morning, they found all those dead bodies! So Sennacherib left Jerusalem and went

BIBLE MYSTERY

Why was it such a "pain in the neck" to lose a battle in Bible times?
Answer: Winners of battles often stood on the necks of the losers to show they had won the battle. See Joshua 10:24.

Did you know that...

when someone broke one of the laws of Assyria they were often punished by having their ears cut off? It paid to listen carefully to the law! It still does.

back to Nineveh. God had kept his promise to Hezekiah. He had defended Jerusalem against the Assyrians.

After the fifteen years passed that God gave to Hezekiah, Hezekiah died, and his son Manasseh became king at age twelve. But Manasseh was not faithful to God as his father had been. He led Judah back to the worship of false gods.

Isaiah's Comfort

During his later years, Isaiah's message from God changed. Most of the ten tribes of Israel were living as captives in foreign countries. And Judah would be cap-

Music

A time of traveling singers, called Rhapsodes, began.

Science, Technology & Growth

- 700 B.C. Scythia, Europe. Saddles for horses were invented by the Scythians, and horseshoes were invented in Europe.
- Assyria. In Nineveh, wells were being dug so that buckets could be used to draw out the water.
- 700 B.C. Ships with two banks of oars were invented.

Daily Life

- 691 B.C. Assyria. A thirty-four-mile aqueduct was built to bring water to Nineveh.
- 688 B.C. Greece. Boxing was added to the Olympic Games.

The Destruction of Sennacherib

The story about how God saved his people from Sennacherib was remembered in this poem by Lord Byron in A.D. 1815.

tured before long. With God's help, Isaiah looked ahead in time and saw when Jesus the Messiah would come to set up his kingdom that would last forever. Then Israel and Judah would be rescued, reunited as one nation, and given a place of peace and joy. It would be a wonderful time for the people God loved and who loved him.

And there lay the steed
　　with his nostril all wide,
But through it there rolled
　　not the breath of his pride;
And the foam of his gasping
　　lay white on the turf,
And cold as the spray of the rock-beating surf.

And there lay the rider distorted and pale,
With the dew on his brow, and the rust on his
　　mail;
And the tents were all silent, the banners alone,
The lances uplifted, the trumpets unblown.

And the widows of Ashur are loud in their wail,
And the idols are broke in the temple of Baal;
And the might of the Gentile, unsmote by the
　　sword,
Hath melted like snow in the glance of the Lord!

The Assyrian came down
　　like the wolf on the fold,
And his cohorts were gleaming
　　in purple and gold;
And the sheen of their spears
　　was like stars on the sea,
When the blue wave rolls
　　nightly on deep Galilee.

"The Lord has made a promise. And by his power he will keep his promise."

Isaiah 62:8

Like the leaves of the forest
　　when Summer is green,
That host with their banners
　　at sunset were seen;
Like the leaves of the forest
　　when Autumn hath blown,
That host on the morrow lay
　　withered and strown.

For the Angel of Death
　　spread his wings on the blast,
And breathed in the face
　　of the foe as he passed;
And the eyes of the sleepers
　　waxed deadly and chill,
And their hearts but once heaved,
　　and forever grew still!

Sennacherib
Invades Judah

Josiah, the Young
King of Judah

Jeremiah the
Weeping Prophet

701 B.C.   639 B.C.   626 B.C.

704 B.C.—King Sennacherib
establishes Nineveh as
the capital of Assyria.
700 B.C.—Iron implements
begin to replace copper
during the Hallstatt
Period in Europe.

664 B.C.—Psamtik I founds
the 26th dynasty and
begins to reunite Egypt.
640 B.C.—Perdiccas I establishes
the Kingdom of Macedonia.

630 B.C.—The Cimmerians
are conquered by the
Scythians in European
Russia.

639 B.C.
Josiah: The Boy King

2 Kings 21–23 and 2 Chronicles 33:1–20

History & Politics

*L*ed by King Manasseh, Judah was once again worshiping false gods and ignoring the true God of heaven. So God brought the army of Assyria to attack Judah again to turn the people back to him. Assyria took Manasseh captive. The Assyrians put a hook in his nose, bronze chains on his hands, and they led him away to Babylon.

There Manasseh prayed to God for help, because he was very sorry for what he had done. God heard Manasseh's prayer and felt sorry for him. So he returned Manasseh to his kingdom in Jerusalem. Then Manasseh knew that God is the Lord, and he tried to lead Judah back to God. He tore down the false gods and destroyed their temples. Then he commanded the people of Judah to worship the true God.

- 690–638 B.C. Judah. Manasseh was King of Judah. He actively supported cult worship, set up Mesopotamian false gods in the Temple of Yahweh in Jerusalem, and practiced child sacrifices.

- Macedonia. The Macedonian kingdom was set up.

119

Literature & Theater

- Greece. The poets, Tyrtaeus and Mimnermus, wrote elegies, love songs, and war songs.
- Judah. The Book of Nahum in the Bible was probably written.
- Assyria. King Ashurbanipal's famous library, with over 25,000 clay tablets that covered history, medicine, astronomy, astrology, and the movement of planets was built.

Religion, Philosophy & Learning

Judah. The worship of Yahweh (God) was revived in Jerusalem by King Josiah.

Visual Arts

Greece. The Acropolis in Athens was begun. Doric sculpture style and life-sized sculptures of women became popular.

Nahum, the Prophet

While Manasseh was helping Judah return to worshiping God, a prophet named Nahum was sent by God with a message against Assyria. At this time Assyria had a cruel and evil king named Ashurbanipal. Nahum went to the city of Nineveh, where Jonah had been about a hundred years before, to tell the people that their city would be destroyed because of their cruelty and evil ways. His message came true in about forty years when Nineveh was completely destroyed.

The Boy King

About that same time, King Manasseh died. His son Amon ruled Judah for about two years. Then Amon's son, Josiah, became King of Judah. He was only eight years old when he became king, but Josiah was the best king Judah had ever had. He always did what God said was right.

When Josiah was sixteen years old, he began to make big changes in Judah. He removed the false gods from Judah and Jerusalem. He destroyed the places for worshiping false gods. He removed the Asherah idols, the wooden and metal idols, and the Baal gods. Then Josiah cut down the incense altars above the idols. He broke up the Asherah idols and the wooden and metal idols. He beat them into powder and sprinkled the powder on the graves of the people who had worshiped those false gods. He burned the bones of their priests on their own altars.

Finally, young King Josiah made the Temple of God in Jerusalem pure again. And he led his people—the people God loved—back to devotion and worship of the one true God of heaven. Josiah was, without a doubt, the greatest king Judah ever had. He was a man like his ancestor, King David, who was the kind of man God wanted.

"There was no king like Josiah before or after him. He obeyed the Lord with all his heart, soul and strength."

2 Kings 23:25

Music

- The seven-stringed lyre was invented.
- 630 B.C. China. A book of songs was put together.

Science, Technology & Growth

- The twelve signs of the Zodiac were first recorded.
- 687 B.C. China. A huge fall of meteors, known as the Lyrid Showers, occurred.

- 650 B.C. The deadly disease, tuberculosis, was first identified. No cure was found until A.D. 1943.
- 650 B.C. Leprosy, a group of harmful skin diseases, was first identified. There is still no complete cure today.

Daily Life

624 B.C. Greece. Horse racing was added to the Olympic Games.

121

Athens: The First Democracy

During the Dark Ages (see page 100), city life in Greece almost disappeared. But as business began to increase through trade, the cities began to grow again.

The largest and most famous Greek city was named Athens. It was located on the Peloponnesian Peninsula. The port of Athens was called Piraeus. Ships from all over the world with trade goods came there to do business with the people of Athens.

Democracy was first used in Athens. Athenians believed that everyone, both rich and poor, should be treated the same under the law. The Assembly in Athens passed the laws. All the citizens—free men over eighteen, but not women or slaves—took part in running the city government by voting on important matters. Our word *politics* comes from the Greek word *politikos*, which means "of the city."

When each citizen takes part in government, it's called a direct democracy. That's what the people had in Athens. Many countries today, like the United States, have representative democracy, where representatives are chosen to express the wishes of groups of people. Philosophy was also popular in Athens. Philosophy means the love of knowledge and wisdom. Three of the great philosophers from Athens were Socrates, Plato, and Aristotle.

The old part of the city of Athens was built high up on a hill. It was called the Acropolis, and it was where a group of temples stood. These buildings included the Parthenon, one of the most famous buildings of ancient Greece. If you visited Athens today, you could still see the ruins of the Parthenon and the Acropolis.

It's a FACT!

The Assyrians were so cruel and evil during this time that they would boil their enemies in oil or skin them alive!

BIBLE MYSTERY

What is the Black Stone of Moab?

Answer: Mesha was the King of Moab. He set up the Moabite Stone about 840 B.C. It celebrated his success in war against Israel. The writing on the stone is about YHWH—the special name given to God in the Old Testament. See 2 Kings 3:4–5.

Josiah, the Young
King of Judah

Jeremiah, the
Weeping Prophet

Josiah Finds the
Book of the Law

639 B.C.

626 B.C.

621 B.C.

640 B.C.—Perdiccas I
establishes the
Kingdom of
Macedonia.

630 B.C.—The
Cimmerians are con-
quered by the
Scythians in European
Russia.

625 B.C.—King Cyaxares
unifies the Median
tribes in Western Asia.

624 B.C.—Horse racing
becomes an event in
the Olympic Games.

Jeremiah: The Prophet Who Cries

The Book of Jeremiah

626 B.C.

During the thirteenth year that King Josiah ruled Judah, God chose another prophet to take his message to them. Like Josiah, this prophet was just a young man when God chose him to be his special messenger. His name was Jeremiah, and he belonged to the family of priests who lived in a small village called Anathoth. Their village was in the land where the tribe of Benjamin had settled.

History & Politics

Babylon. The Assyrians destroyed Babylon and changed the course of the Euphrates River until it covered the city of Babylon with water.

Euphrates River

God Calls Jeremiah

God said to Jeremiah, "Before I made you in your mother's womb, I chose you. Before you were born, I set you apart for a special work. I appointed you as a prophet to the nations."

But Jeremiah said to God, "But Lord God, I don't know how to speak. I am only a boy."

123

- Sicily. Ballads about great heroes were being written by Stesichorus.

- Judah. The Bible books of Jeremiah, and Zephaniah were probably written.

Religion, Philosophy & Learning

630–553 B.C. Persia. Zoroaster began a new, one-god religion that worshiped the false god Ahura-Mazda.

Then God said, "Don't say, 'I am only a boy.' You must go everywhere that I send you. You must say everything I tell you to say. Don't be afraid of anyone, because I am with you. I will protect you." Then God reached out and touched Jeremiah's mouth and said, "See, I am putting my words in your mouth."

Jeremiah's Two Dreams

God gave Jeremiah two dreams. In the first dream Jeremiah saw a stick of almond wood. And God said, "This means that I am watching to make sure my words come true." (The Hebrew word for "watching" sounds like the Hebrew word for "almond tree.")

In the second dream Jeremiah saw a pot of boiling water that was tipping over from the north. To the people of Jeremiah's time, a boiling pot stood for war. Then God explained that the pot of boiling water meant that disaster would come to Judah from the north.

Jeremiah's Troubles

For the next fifty years, Jeremiah spoke God's message against Judah and Jerusalem. All the other priests were wrongly saying they were going to have peace. So the people chose not to believe Jeremiah. They didn't want to hear his warning about the war and trouble. They treated Jeremiah cruelly. And they stood up against him and his message—the warning from God.

During this time the strong nations around them were at war. Assyria, Babylonia, and Egypt were all fighting each other. After several years, Babylon and their king, Nebuchadnezzar, were the winners. Sadly for Judah, it was Babylon that would be the boiling pot of water in Jeremiah's dream. Babylon would take Judah captive.

Visual Arts

Greece. Houses were designed with more fancy decoration on them.

Music

Terpander wrote music for a solo voice to sing with instruments playing.

"The time is coming when I will make a new agreement… with the people of Israel. I will put my teachings in their minds. And I will write them on their hearts."

Jeremiah 31:31–33

Science, Technology & Growth

Kaleus was the first to sail a ship through the Straits of Gibraltar.

Daily Life

Greece. Ornamental weaving was being done.

Who Was Zoroaster?

One of the strong empires during the time of Jeremiah and Josiah was Persia. Like many other people, the Persians worshiped many false gods. About 600 B.C. a priest named Zoroaster (also called Zarathustra) changed Persia's religion. He sets up a single false god called Ahura-Mazda. He says that this false god made everything in the world and that no other gods except him are right.

Zoroaster knew a lot about religion. His new religion was based on people's free will to worship the one false god, Ahura-Mazda. The other religions worshiped many gods and were ruled by special ceremonies, animal sacrifices, and drugs. So Zoroaster replaced Persia's polytheism (the worship of many gods) with monotheism (the worship of one god).

Zoroaster believed that Ahura-Mazda was the only true god and was ruler of everything. So he also taught that people did not have to obey the laws of Persia if the laws were unfair and unjust.

He also believed that good and evil were like twin spirits, and Ahura-Mazda was their father. He taught that the world is a battleground where Ahura-Mazda (good) fights evil. And he believed that good would win the battle in the end.

This religion came to be known by its inventor's name. It was called Zoroasterism. But it was a false religion because it did not worship the real God of heaven.

Good News

Most of Jeremiah's message to Judah was sad, but you can read happy news in his words, too. Through Jeremiah God said that he was going to make a new agreement with Judah and Israel. He said he would forgive their sins and put his new law in their hearts. God was telling his people the good news about the time when Jesus would come to save them!

DID YOU KNOW THAT...

Jeremiah is called the "weeping prophet," because he cried for Judah and Israel's sinful ways.

BIBLE MYSTERY

Which teenage king was a real dirt digger?
Answer: Uzziah. He loved the earth and had many farms and vineyards. See 2 Chronicles 26:10.

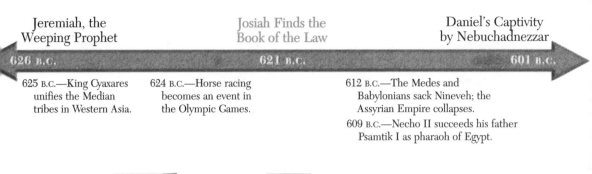

Jeremiah, the
Weeping Prophet

Josiah Finds the
Book of the Law

Daniel's Captivity
by Nebuchadnezzar

626 B.C.

621 B.C.

601 B.C.

625 B.C.—King Cyaxares
unifies the Median
tribes in Western Asia.

624 B.C.—Horse racing
becomes an event in
the Olympic Games.

612 B.C.—The Medes and
Babylonians sack Nineveh; the
Assyrian Empire collapses.

609 B.C.—Necho II succeeds his father
Psamtik I as pharaoh of Egypt.

The Treasure Is Found!

621 B.C.

2 Kings 22–23

It was the eighteenth year of King Josiah's rule over Judah. Jeremiah was still speaking God's message of doom to Judah. And King Josiah commanded that the Temple of God in Jerusalem be repaired. He told the Levites to take the money brought to the Temple to buy supplies and pay the workers.

Book of the Teaching

While they were bringing the money out of the Temple, Hilkiah the priest found the long lost Book of the Teachings of the Lord that had been given to Moses. What a treasure! Hilkiah gave the book to Shaphan, the royal assistant, who read it.

History & Politics

- Syria, Palestine. Scythian raiders attacked these two countries.
- 620 B.C. Greece. Scribes wrote Greek laws in stone in public places for all the people to read. These were done in the busiest parts of the cities so the most people would see them.

Literature & Theater

Greece. Arion, a famous Greek poet and composer, introduced strophe and antistrophe.

Religion, Philosophy & Learning

- Greece. Good elementary education was being offered in Nubia.

- Judah. The Book of the Teachings of God were found in the Temple in Jerusalem after having been lost for decades.

Visual Arts

Babylon. King Nebuchadnezzar sponsored works of art and great architecture.

Then Shaphan went to see King Josiah and said, "Hilkiah the priest has given me a book." And Shaphan read from the Book to the king. When the king heard God's words from the Book of the Teachings, he knew it was God's holy words and that Judah had not obeyed them. So he tore his clothes to show how upset he was.

King Josiah sent Shaphan and some other men to ask the Lord about the words in the Book of the Teachings. So Shaphan, his son Ahikam, Acbor, and Asaiah went to see Huldah, a prophet of God. They asked her what the Lord's words meant.

Huldah told the men that God was angry with Judah for worshiping other gods and not following his words. She said that he was going to bring trouble to Judah, and that his anger could not be stopped. She also said that God had seen Josiah's sadness because Judah had not obeyed him. And God would let Josiah die, rather than have to watch Jerusalem and Judah be destroyed. And that's the message that Shaphan and the others took back to King Josiah.

The People Hear the Teachings

When King Josiah heard what God had said, he gathered all the people of Judah at the Temple of the Lord. There he read to them all the words of God from the Book of the Teachings. Then King Josiah made a solemn promise to God that he would obey all the Teachings of the Book. And the people promised to obey them, too.

After that, King Josiah destroyed everything in all the land that honored

There was no king like Josiah before or after him. He obeyed the Lord with all his heart, soul and strength. He followed all the Teachings of Moses."

2 Kings 23:25

Music

620 B.C. —Greece. Alcaeus, author of political, love, and war songs was living and working.

Science, Technology & Growth

Egypt. Necho II, King of Egypt, started building a canal between the Nile River and the Red Sea.

Daily Life

620 B.C. Greece. Traders began using metal coins for business dealings.

Buying and Selling

Today, when we want to buy something, we just trade money for what we want. But in the earliest days of civilization, people didn't have money. So they bought and sold things through a system called "bartering" or trading.

Bartering. In the bartering system, people swapped what they had for what they needed. For instance, Farmer Jones might trade tomatoes and corn for Farmer Brown's wheat and eggs. Sometimes, instead of goods, people traded time for things they needed. Farmer Jones might offer to trade one whole day of work for two bushels of Farmer Brown's beans.

Gold dust. Bartering worked well until traders began traveling long distances. Then they needed a more convenient way to exchange goods and do business with each other. At first, they tried using loose, powdered gold. The gold was weighed on a set of scales. So, instead of paying "two dollars" for a new shirt, perhaps they paid "one-half ounce" of gold for the shirt.

Gold and silver coins. Weighing the gold was a lot of trouble. So, people began to make coins out of the gold. Each coin contained a set amount of gold and was worth an exact amount. The first coins were made out of electrum, which was a mixture of gold and silver.

Paper money. Still, gold coins were very heavy to carry around. So, finally, people began making paper money. And each piece of paper money stood for a certain

any god except the God of heaven. He destroyed their places of worship to false gods, their false priests and prophets, their idols, their places of sacrifice, their fortune-tellers and witches, and anything else that had to do with the evil they had begun to do.

DID YOU KNOW THAT...

Josiah was king for 31 long years, but when he died in battle, he was still only 39 years old?

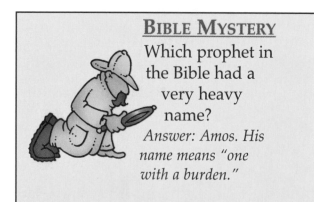

BIBLE MYSTERY

Which prophet in the Bible had a very heavy name?

Answer: Amos. His name means "one with a burden."

Finally, King Josiah commanded the people to celebrate the Passover feast—the feast God began when he rescued Israel from slavery in Egypt.

The Bible says, "There was no king like Josiah before or after him. He obeyed the Lord with all his heart, soul and strength. He followed all the Teachings of Moses."

amount of gold that was kept on deposit in a storage place, such as a bank.

Today we have both paper money and different sizes of coins. And today lots of people still like to barter, too. For instance, a music teacher might give a boy music lessons in exchange for his mowing the lawn. It's the best of both worlds!.

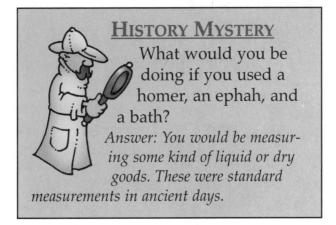

HISTORY MYSTERY

What would you be doing if you used a homer, an ephah, and a bath?

Answer: You would be measuring some kind of liquid or dry goods. These were standard measurements in ancient days.

612 B.C.—The Medes and Babylonians sack Nineveh; the Assyrian Empire collapses.

609 B.C.—Necho II succeeds his father Psamtik I as pharaoh of Egypt.

600 B.C.—Building of a Doric temple begins at the Olympia in Greece.

600 B.C.—The false religion of Zoroastrianism develops in Iran.

601 B.C.

Daniel and the Dream

Daniel 1–2

History & Politics

Mexico. The Mayan civilization existed.

Literature & Theater

- 600 B.C. Greece. Sappho a well-known poetess, lived and wrote on the island of Lesbos.

- 605 B.C. Judah. The Bible prophet, Jeremiah, dictated his prophecies of twenty-three years to his secretary, Baruch.

A price always has to be paid for sin. King Josiah had brought Judah back to God, but the people still had to pay the price for the horrible sins they had done earlier under Manasseh. And the time for them to pay the price had come, just as Jeremiah the prophet had said it would.

Taken Captive!

Egypt and Babylon had one of the worst battles in history. Babylon defeated Egypt and then took Judah captive. Many people from Judah, including a young man named Daniel, were taken to Babylon as slaves. Soon several young men from Judah were cho-

sen for special service in King Nebuchadnezzar's palace. One of those men was Daniel, along with his friends Shadrach, Meshach, and Abednego.

The King's Dream

One night King Nebuchadnezzar had a dream. The dream troubled the king, and he couldn't sleep. So he called for his wise men to come and tell him what the dream meant.

The king said to Daniel, "Truly I know your God is the greatest of all gods. And he is the Lord of all the kings. He tells people about things they cannot know. I know this is true. You were able to tell these secret things to me."

Daniel 2:47

Religion, Philosophy & Learning

Greece. This was the "Age of the Seven Wise Men of Greece." The seven wise men were named Thales, Pittacus, Bias, Solon, Cleobulus, Periander, and Chilo. These seven men were philosophers.

Visual Arts

600 B.C. Greece. Greek art became independent from other cultures. Their architecture changed from the hard lines of the Doric style to the softer, more graceful lines of the Ionic style of art.

Music

Greece. Pythagoras invented the eight-note octave.

Science, Technology & Growth

- 605–562 B.C. Babylonia. King Nebuchadnezzar built the world-famous Hanging Gardens. These gardens are one of the Seven Wonders of the Ancient World. They were built on the roof of the king's palace in terraces, had many exotic plants, and were watered with artificial irrigation.
- Chios. An inventor named Glaucus introduced the process of soldering iron.

Daily Life

- 600 B.C. Italy. Olive trees were brought to Italy from Greece for the first time.
- India. Elephants were first used in war.
- Greece. Boys were being trained for manhood by hunting wild boars.

The wise men said, "Tell us your dream, O King, and we will tell you what it means."

But the king said, "No. You must tell me what dream I dreamed and what it means. Or you will die."

But the wise men could not tell the king what dream he had dreamed. So Nebuchadnezzar had them all killed.

Then Daniel came to see the king. God helped Daniel tell the king what dream he had dreamed and what it

BIBLE MYSTERY

What were Shadrach, Meshach, and Abednego's real names?
Answer: Shadrach's Hebrew name was Hananiah; Meshach's was Mishael; and Abednego's was Azariah. Ashpenaz, chief officer to King Nebuchadnezzar gave them Babylonian names.

meant. He said that the king had dreamed about a huge statue that was made of gold, silver, bronze, iron, and clay. He explained that each of those metals stood for a kingdom that would rule in the future.

Then he said that the king had dreamed that a rock was thrown at the feet of the statue, the statue was broken into pieces, and the wind blew it away. Daniel said that meant that God would send a kingdom someday that would destroy all the other kingdoms, but God's kingdom would never be destroyed. (He was talking about the kingdom of Jesus!)

Daniel Rewarded

The king was amazed! He fell down on his face in front of Daniel and praised God. Then the king put Daniel in an important job in Babylon. He became

DID YOU KNOW THAT...

Daniel's Babylonian name was Belteshazzar? They made him change his Hebrew name when he was taken captive.

Let There Be Light

The Bible says that goodness loves light, but evil loves darkness. So people have always tried to develop ways to light the darkness, even in earliest times.

Sun and moon. The first came from God. He said, "Let there be light!" And the sun and moon appeared. After that, people began finding ways to make artificial (fake) light.

Oil lamps. Fire was the first artificial light, but it was dangerous and hard to carry around. Then people found out they could get light by burning oil, and the first lamps

were invented. These lamps were simply hollowed-out rocks full of animal fat.

About 1000 B.C. lamps were made with wicks of vegetable fibers. The lamps had a small channel or spout to hold the wick. Oil from the bowl of the lamp soaked up to the end of the wick. Then the wick was set on fire to make light.

Candle power. By the time Jesus was born (the first century), candles were being made. A candle is just a wick surrounded by wax or tallow. When the wick is lit, the flame melts some of the wax or tallow, which burns to give off light. So the candle is really just an oil lamp in a form that's easier to use.

ruler over all of Babylon, and he was put in charge of all the wise men. The king also appointed Shadrach, Meshach, and Abednego to be rulers over the land under Daniel.

Nebuchadnezzar was amazed at what Daniel's God could do, but he didn't totally believe in God. And he didn't stop making Judah serve him as slaves.

Daniel's Captivity by Nebuchadnezzar	Great Deportation	Ezekiel Prophesies
01 B.C.	597 B.C.	592 B.C.

600 B.C.—The Greek colony of Poseidonia (Pæstum) is founded in Italy.

600 B.C.—The Greeks found Massilia (Marseilles) on the Mediterranean coast.

594 B.C.—The archon Solon makes sweeping social reforms in Athens.

Deported To Babylon

597 B.C.

Jeremiah 36
2 Kings 24

After good King Josiah died, his son Jehoahaz ruled for a short time. Then Josiah's son Jehoiakim became king of Judah. Jehoiakim was not good like his father, and he brought false gods back into Judah. So Jeremiah the prophet continued to warn Judah about the coming captivity.

Jeremiah's Scroll

During Jehoiakim's rule, God told Jeremiah to write down all the prophecies he had spoken in the twenty-three years he had been delivering God's messages. So Jeremiah dictated all his past prophecies to his secretary—a man named Baruch. It was a long, hard job to prepare the scroll of Jeremiah's prophecies, and Baruch was happy when they were finished.

History & Politics

Corsica. The Phoenicians invaded Corsica.

Literature & Theater

- Greece. Papyrus was first used as writing material.
- Greece. Alcman and Arion lived and wrote poetry and music.

Religion, Philosophy & Learning

597 B.C. Judah. Zedekiah, the last king of Judah, began his reign.

Visual Arts

Greece. Sculptures showing people in long, draped clothing became popular.

Music

600 B.C. Assyria. Orchestras played music for state events. The musical instruments included

harps, double-reed pipes, and a drum. A choir of fifteen women also sang.

When the scroll was finished, Jeremiah told Baruch to take it to the Temple of God and read it out loud. Reading the scroll reminded the people of Judah of all the warnings they had received from God. Then Baruch read it to the king's officers. When they heard the words of God in the scroll, they were afraid. And they told Baruch and Jeremiah to hide from King Jehoiakim.

The officers read the scroll of Jeremiah to King Jehoiakim. But Jehoiakim did not listen to the words of God. Instead, he cut the scroll into pieces and burned it. And he told the officers to arrest Baruch and Jeremiah, but God had hidden them, and they could not be found.

After that, God told Jeremiah to dictate all his prophecies to Baruch

BIBLE MYSTERY
What was King Zedekiah's name before he became king of Judah?
Answer: His name was Mattaniah. King Nebuchadnezzar gave him a Babylonian name when he appointed him king. See 2 Kings 24:17.

again. So they prepared a second scroll, which was kept safe from Jehoiakim.

Deported!

After Babylon took Judah captive, King Jehoiakim died, and his son Jehoiachin became king. But he only ruled for three months. Then King Nebuchadnezzar sent Jehoiachin away to Babylon as a captive, and he appointed King Josiah's third son, Zedekiah, as King of Judah.

It was at that time that many more people from Judah were deported from Judah to Babylon as captives. More

"The Lord corrects those he loves, just as a father corrects the child that he likes."

Proverbs 3:12

- 600-300 B.C. Egypt. Instruments for surveying land were invented. They invented the groma to set out squares and rectangles. This was a simple cross of wood held horizontally. Plumb lines hanging from each stick allowed surveyors to sight along lines at exact right angles.
- Rome. T. Priscus built the first Roman stone bridge.

Daily Life

Greece. Civil rights for women decreased and education for boys began.

Alcman and Arion

In the country of Greece about this time were two famous poets named Alcman and Arion.

Alcman is thought to be from Lydia in Anatolia. He lived in the Greek city of Sparta and wrote poems in the Doric dialect. He was really good in "partheneia," which were hymns sung by choirs of young girls.

In Greece, poetry, dance, and music were performed for the young people. But they were also important parts of religious and political life.

Arion was a poet and lyre player. He was a student of Alcman. And once he came close to being killed. Arion traveled from city to city performing his choral lyrics. He even made a tour of Italy, where his singing and playing brought him much money, and he became rich.

On his return trip to Greece, the sailors tried to murder Arion and steal his money. He was given his wish to sing one last time before they killed him. After he sang, he threw himself overboard! As the legend goes, a dolphin, attracted to Arion's music, carried him safely to the shore on his back.

people were deported this time than ever before or after. And one of the people deported was a man named Ezekiel.

It's a FACT!

In the Bible there are about 773,692 words. That's about 3,566,480 letters! Imagine how tired Baruch would have been if he had written the whole Bible, instead of just the Book of Jeremiah.

Discipline and Love

Once again God's words had come true. The people of Judah were being punished for the evil things they had done. God was punishing them because he loved them so much, and he wanted them to come back to him. It was just as wise King Solomon had once said: "The Lord corrects those he loves, just as a father corrects the child that he likes."

Great Deportation	Ezekiel Prophesies	Babylonia Captures Jerusalem
597 B.C.	592 B.C.	588–586 B.C.

594 B.C.—Solon makes sweeping social reforms in Athens.

585 B.C.—Greek philosopher and scientist, Thales of Miletus, predicts an eclipse of the sun.

Dance of the Dry Bones

592 B.C.

The Book of Ezekiel

God's people were separated. Many of them had been taken to Babylon as captives; the rest were still in Judah. During this time God had two prophets: Jeremiah and Ezekiel. Jeremiah continued to deliver God's messages to the people of Judah in Jerusalem, while Ezekiel began speaking to the people of Judah who were captives in Babylon.

God spoke to Ezekiel in very unusual ways. Ezekiel often had strange dreams and saw visions from God. In these dreams God told Ezekiel what to say to the people. One of the most exciting dreams was about dry bones.

History & Politics

594 B.C. Greece. The Greek ruler, Solon, made many social changes in Athens.

Literature & Theater

- Greece. A poet named Thespis held the first public performance of his tragedy based on a hymn to Dionysus. This was the beginning of drama. Actors started being called "Thespians" after Thespis.

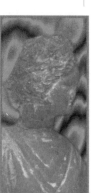

- The Book of Ezekiel in the Bible was probably written.

Religion, Philosophy & Learning

593 B.C. Ezekiel, the biblical prophet, saw his first vision during a great storm.

Visual Arts

600 B.C. Greece. The great temple at Olympia was built.

Music

"Modes" in music were developed.

Dream of Dry Bones

Ezekiel dreamed that God took him to a valley that was full of bones. The bones were very dry. Then God asked Ezekiel, "Can these bones live?" And Ezekiel said that only God knew if the bones could live.

The Lord told Ezekiel to speak to the dry bones and tell them this: "I will cause breath to enter you. Then you will live. I will put muscles on you. I will put flesh on you. I will cover you with skin. Then I will put breath in you, and you will live. Then you will know that I am the Lord."

So Ezekiel began to speak the words of God to the dry bones. While he was speaking to them, Ezekiel heard a rattling noise. Then he saw the bones come together, and muscles started forming on the bones. Next, flesh grew, and skin covered the bones. But they were still not alive.

After that, God told Ezekiel to speak to the wind and say this: "Wind, breathe on these people who were killed so they can live again." And Ezekiel spoke to the wind as God had told him to do. Then breath came into the flesh-covered bones, and they came to life! They stood up on their feet. And when Ezekiel looked, the dry bones had become a large army of living people.

God said to Ezekiel, "Human being, stand up on your feet. Then I will speak with you… I am sending you to the people of Israel."

Ezekiel 2:1-3

Science, Technology & Growth

- 600 B.C. Austria. The winch (or windlass) was discovered. The main purpose of the winch was to give workers more lifting power when hauling things up on a rope. It was an important part of the crane.

  The Greek doctor, Hippocrates, is said to have used a winch for stretching people's arms and legs!

- Phoenicia. The Phoenicians first sailed around the southern end of Africa. Their trip began at the Red Sea and lasted three years. As they came around the point of Africa, sailors noticed that now the sun rose on a different side of the ship.

What Are the Thespians?

The word thespian *means "actor." It is taken from the name Thespis, who was a famous poet in Greece. According to tradition, Thespis, who lived about the same time as Ezekiel, was the person who founded drama.*

Thespis was born in the city of Attica. He wrote many plays, and he won a prize for a play he wrote about 534 B.C. That kind of play is called a "tragedy," because it tells the story of something sad. The other kind of play is called a "comedy," which tells the story of something funny.

Thespis is thought to be the first playwright to have an actor, who was not in the chorus, make speeches. The actor also had conversations with the leader of the chorus. This was a new way of presenting plays in the theater. And most people agree that this was the beginning of real drama.

Thespis is famous for something else, too. He probably was the one who began using masks to disguise the actors on stage.

Today, professional actors often become members of groups of actors. Those groups are sometimes called "Thespian Players," in honor of Thespis, who began drama so many hundreds of years ago.

What the Dry Bones Meant

Then God explained the dream to Ezekiel. He said that he was going to bring life back to Judah—the people he loved so much. And he would bring them out of captivity and back to their homeland. Then Judah would know that their return to Israel was a gift from God and that it wasn't because of anything or anybody else.

Did you know that...

Ezekiel was an actor? Once he lay down on his left side for 390 days! He was acting out God's message that Jerusalem would be attacked. See Ezekiel 4:1-17.

Ezekiel Prophesies	Babylonia Captures Jerusalem	Shadrach, Meshach, and Abednego
592 B.C.	588–586 B.C.	584 B.C.

594 B.C.—Solon makes sweeping social reforms in Athens.

585 B.C.—Greek philosopher and scientist, Thales of Miletus, predicts an eclipse of the sun.

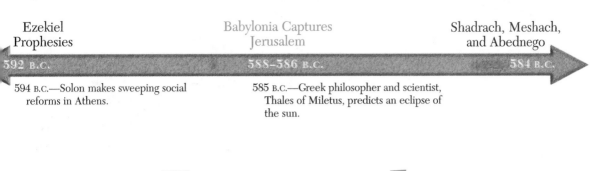

588–586 B.C. Jerusalem Destroyed!

Ezekiel 24–28
Jeremiah 21–31, 37–38
2 Kings 25

*D*uring the days of Ezekiel and Jeremiah, King Zedekiah of Judah made a big mistake. He turned against King Nebuchadnezzar of Babylon. When he did, Nebuchadnezzar brought his strong army and surrounded all the cities of Judah, including Jerusalem, the Holy City of God.

Surrounded!

Nebuchadnezzar's army set up camp all around Jerusalem. Then they built seigeworks against the walls of the city. Seigeworks were ramps of dirt that led to the top of the city walls, like roads. The army could run up the ramps and over the walls to attack the city.

History & Politics

589 B.C. Judah. King Zedekiah rebelled against King Nebuchadnezzar of Babylon. This set off Babylon's attack on Jerusalem and, eventually, the complete destruction of the Holy City.

145

Literature & Theater

- Ephesus. Hipponax was writing political satire, a kind of writing that pokes fun at rulers and government officers. He invented a style of poetry called "lame iambics" for this purpose.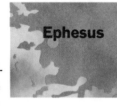
- The Bible books of Lamentations and Obadiah were probably written.

Religion, Philosophy & Learning

- 586 B.C. Judah. The Temple of God and Solomon's Great Palace were burned in Jerusalem by the Babylonian army.
- Babylon. The people of Judah began their slavery in Babylon.
- Edom. The prophet Obadiah was bringing God's message against Edom.

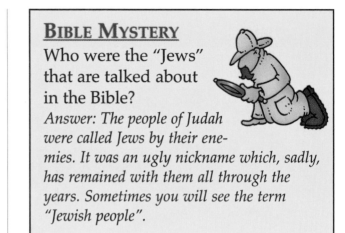

BIBLE MYSTERY

Who were the "Jews" that are talked about in the Bible?

Answer: The people of Judah were called Jews by their enemies. It was an ugly nickname which, sadly, has remained with them all through the years. Sometimes you will see the term "Jewish people".

By surrounding the city, Babylon's army cut off all food from coming into Jerusalem. Before long, there was no food at all left in the city, and everyone was very hungry.

A Breakthrough

Then Babylon's army broke through one of the city walls. When that happened, King Zedekiah and his whole army ran out one of the city gates, trying to escape. They ran toward the Jordan Valley, but the Babylonian army chased them and caught them in the plains of Jericho.

Zedekiah's army was scattered and could not fight back. So Babylon's army captured Zedekiah and took him to King Nebuchadnezzar. The king made Zedekiah watch as they killed his sons. Then they put out Zedekiah's eyes so that his sons' deaths were the last thing he ever saw. Finally, they put bronze chains on Zedekiah and took him to Babylon as a slave.

Jerusalem Destroyed

Nebuzaradan, commander of Nebuchadnezzar's special guards, went to Jerusalem and set fire to the Temple of God and the king's palace. He also burned all the houses and every important building in Jerusalem.

Visual Arts

Burma. The Shwe Dagon Pagoda, a very beautiful oriental building, was built.

Music

Greece. Choral music was being sung.

"So the people of Judah were led away from their country as captives."

2 Kings 25:21

147

The Babylonian army broke down all the walls around Jerusalem and took the people of Jerusalem captive. But they left behind some of the poorest people of Judah to take care of the vineyards and fields.

Babylonian soldiers also took all the beautiful things used for service to God in the Temple and carried them back to Babylon. They took everything made of gold, silver, and bronze.

DID YOU KNOW THAT...

there was so much bronze in the Temple of God that it couldn't even be weighed! See 2 Kings 25:16.

HISTORY MYSTERY

What was special about a sheep's liver in the days of Nebuchadnezzar?

Answer: The Babylonians believed they could tell the future by looking at a sheep's liver. Clay models of a sheep's liver have been found showing the different parts of the liver and what they meant.

The Holy City of God—the City of David—had fallen to Babylon... and its fall was very great. The prophecies of Jeremiah, Ezekiel, and the other prophets had come true. And yet, through it all, God loved his people and wanted them to come back to him with their hearts. So, soon he would show them a way out.

Choral Music

During the times of Jeremiah and Ezekiel, choral music was being developed in Greece. Choral music is sung by a group of people as a unit. Usually choral music means there are two or more singers for each voice part (soprano, alto, tenor, and bass). When there is only one singer on each voice part, it's called a part-song.

Most choral music is written for a chorus, or choir, perhaps made up of women and men. But some choirs are only boys and men. Others are only women or children.

In ancient Greece, religious feelings were expressed in drama by a chorus. (See also "What Are the Thespians"? on page 144.) Although the chorus members were dancers and actors, as well as singers, after a while the word chorus came to mean only singers.

Since this early beginning, choral music has developed in many different ways. Today, choirs often specialize in certain kinds of songs and certain types of singing. Some choirs sing while musical instruments play with them. Other choirs sing a cappella—without instruments playing. Some choirs sing hymns, while others sing spirituals, and others sing jazz. Each kind of song may be religious or not, depending on the words of the songs.

In the New Testament we are told by God to "Sing psalms, hymns, and spiritual songs with thankfulness in your hearts to God" (Colossians 3:16). So it's not the kind of songs we sing, but the attitude of our hearts, that make God happy with our worship.

Babylonia Captures Jerusalem	Shadrach, Meshach and Abednego	Ezekiel's Temple Vision
588–586 B.C.	584 B.C.	572 B.C

585 B.C.—Greek philosopher and scientist, Thales of Miletus, predicts
an eclipse of the sun.

570 B.C.—Ahmose II
becomes king of Egypt.

570 B.C.—Cleitias, a Greek
vase painter of the Black
Figure style, is active.

584 B.C.

Four Men in a Fire

Daniel 3:1-30

History & Politics

• 584 B.C. A group of people in Judah ran away from the Babylonian army to Egypt. They forced Jeremiah the prophet and his secretary, Baruch, to go with them. They settled in the fortress city of Tahpanhes on the border.

• Mayan people settle in Mexico.

Back in Babylon where the people of Judah were slaves, Daniel was second in command to King Nebuchadnezzar himself. When this story happened, Daniel was probably away from the city on business for the king. If he had been there, he surely would have tried to help his friends.

The Golden Statue

King Nebuchadnezzar didn't really know or worship the true God, even though he had seen God's power work when Daniel told him his dream. So he had a huge golden statue set up near the city of Babylon.

Then the king called all the people together. He said that when they heard the sound of musical instruments, they were to bow down and worship the giant false god. If they did not worship the statue, they would be thrown into a blazing furnace!

Everyone bowed down to the statue except Shadrach, Meshach, and Abednego—the rulers of Babylon who served under Daniel. They would not bow down to any god except the true God of heaven.

The King Becomes Angry

King Nebuchadnezzar became angry! He ordered the furnace heated seven times hotter than usual. Then the three young men were tied up and thrown into the white-hot furnace.

HISTORY MYSTERY
What is the name we call the ancient country of Babylon today?
Answer: Iraq.

- The great theater at Delphi was built.
- Æsop's Fables were written.

Religion, Philosophy & Learning

Babylon. While Nebuchadnezzar held God's people captive in Babylon, many books of the Old Testament, based on stories handed down by word of mouth, were first written down in the language of Hebrew.

Music

India. The Indian vina was invented. Made of two hollow gourds joined by strings and bamboo reed, it was probably the first hollow stringed instrument, like guitars and violins today.

Science, Technology, & Growth

Babylon. King Nebuchadnezzar built the famous Hanging Gardens in the palace at

Babylon. These gardens are one of the seven wonders of the world. Shadrach, Meshach, and Abednego surely saw the gardens, or perhaps they even worked to help build them.

Daily Life

Greece. The amazing athlete, Milo of Crotona, won six crowns during the Olympic Games.

The One True God

Suddenly the king saw something amazing. Four men, not three, were walking around in the fire! They were not tied up, and they were not even burned. The king had them brought out of the fiery furnace. Their clothes didn't even smell like smoke. It was fantastic!

King Nebuchadnezzar said, "Praise the God of Shadrach, Meshach, and Abednego. Their God has sent his angel to save them from the fire!"

Then the king made a new law that said no one could speak against God because, he said, "No other god can save his people like this God."

Mind Meld

"No other god can save his people like this God."

Daniel 3:29

Once again, King Nebuchadnezzar was shown the mighty power of God. But once again, he did not really believe in God or follow him. Someday, though, if the king continued seeing God's awesome power in action, he might really believe in God with all his heart.

It's a
FACT!
The gold statue King Nebuchadnezzar built was ninety feet tall and nine feet wide.
Wow!

BIBLE MYSTERY
What river ran through the Garden of Eden and also ran near Babylon?
Answer: The Euphrates.

Æsop's Fables

As boys, Shadrach, Meshach, and Abednego probably listened to Æsop's Fables. Æsop was a Phrygian slave who wrote wonderful tales about animals that behaved like people in made-up stories. Each story taught a lesson (or moral) about how people should live. One of Æsop's most famous fables is about a mouse that helped a lion. Æsop died in 585 B.C., but we still read his fables today.

The Lion and the Mouse
by Æsop

A lion was lying asleep when a mouse ran over his face and woke him up! The lion was angry. He caught the little mouse and was about to kill him. But the mouse cried out, "If you will not kill me, I will repay your kindness some day."

The lion laughed at the idea of a mouse helping a lion and let the mouse go. Soon the lion was caught by hunters. They tied him to the ground with strong ropes. The lion roared! The mouse heard him and came to where the lion was tied. With his teeth the mouse gnawed the rope in two and freed the lion.

Then the mouse said, "You laughed at the idea of my helping you. You never thought I could repay your favor. But now you know that even a little mouse can sometimes help a big lion."

Moral: Don't look down on others.

Shadrach, Meshach, and Abednego

Ezekiel's Temple Vision

Nebuchadnezzar's Insanity

584 B.C.

572 B.C.

562 B.C.

585 B.C.—Greek philosopher and scientist, Thales of Miletus, predicts an eclipse of the sun.

570 B.C.—Ahmose II becomes king of Egypt.

570 B.C.—Cleitias, a Greek vase painter of the Black Figure style, is active.

561 B.C.— Peisistratus becomes tyrant of Athens.

572 B.C.

The Great Temple Dream

The Book of Lamentations Ezekiel 40-48

History & Politics

- 570 B.C. Egypt. Ahmose II became king.
- 585-572 B.C. Phoenicia. The city of Tyre was surrounded by the Babylonian army for thirteen years before it surrendered. When that happened, Phoenicia stopped being a nation forever.
- Cyprus was under Egyptian rule.

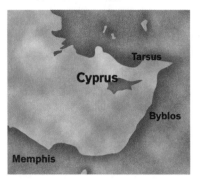

Tarsus

Cyprus

Byblos

Memphis

Jeremiah had been right. Jerusalem was destroyed. Should he laugh and say, "I told you so"? No. Jeremiah was heartbroken that his city and his people were shamed and separated. His family and friends had been taken away to Babylon as captives. His hometown of Jerusalem was a pile of rubble. And even he was in a foreign country.

So, once again, this great prophet of God cried for Judah. He wrote of his sadness in a beautiful poem. His sad thoughts are called "laments." You can read Jeremiah's poem in the Book of Lamentations in your Bible.

154

From Despair to Hope

Meanwhile, back in Babylon, the prophet Ezekiel was still with the people of Judah in slavery. When the news arrived about the Fall of Jerusalem, Ezekiel's message from God changed from despair to hope. He began telling the people that God was going to gather up his people from the places they had been taken and return them to the Promised Land—Canaan, which was later called Palestine. He also reminded them that God was still planning to send the Messiah, the Savior, to rescue them one day.

HISTORY MYSTERY
Who invented the lock and key?
Answer: Theodorus of Samos.

Literature & Theater

580-542 B.C. Greece. A famous Greek poet named Anacreon lived and wrote.

Religion, Philosophy & Learning

- 581-497 B.C. The famous philosopher and mathematician, Pythagoras, lived and worked.
- 586-526 B.C. Greece. Anaximenes of the city of Miletus lived and taught as a philosopher.

Visual Arts

570 B.C. Greece. A painter named Cleitias began using the Black Figure style of vase painting.

Science, Technology & Growth

Samos. An inventor named Theodorus developed these things: ore smelting and casting; the carpenter's square; the turning lathe; and other things.

Daily Life

Greece. Women began to wear the men's short chiton as a long dress of their own.

The New Temple

About twelve years later, God gave Ezekiel another amazing dream. He showed him a grand new temple. God showed Ezekiel all the details of the new temple, just as he had once described the Holy Tent built in the desert and Solomon's Temple that had recently been destroyed in Jerusalem.

Although some things about the new temple were to be like the first two, many things about the new one were to be different. Ezekiel's dream showed a man of bronze measuring the new temple. His measurements

Mind Meld

Ezekiel said, "I bowed facedown on the ground. The greatness of the Lord came into the Temple through the east gate."

Ezekiel 43:3b-4

DID YOU KNOW THAT...

Greek philosophers
at this time thought
the earth was a flat disk
(like a plate)
and it was covered
with a dome of sky?
They didn't know
they could go
"around the world"
as we do.

showed that the new temple would be much larger than the old one, and that was good news. But a much larger temple meant that it would take a lot longer

The Caste System

In 575 B.C. in the country of India, people were divided into four main social groups, called "castes." People were assigned to castes when they were born. They were not allowed to marry someone in another caste. And it was supposed to be impossible to change from one caste to another.

This social system was closely related to the Indian's main religion—Hinduism. The Hindu people worshiped thousands of false gods and goddesses. Their priests sang long hymns to the people from memory. And more than a thousand of these hymns were collected by a man named Punjab to become the Hindu sacred book called Rig-Veda.

Here are the four castes of India at that time and what each one was allowed to do.

Brahmans were Hindu priests and scholars. They were thought to have godly power. Their job was to study and teach the Rig-Veda. They also offered sacrifices, such as food, to the false gods.

Kshatriya were the Hindu warriors. Their main job was to fight wars for the people. They also had the right to offer sacrifices and to study the Rig-Veda.

Vaisyas were the merchants, farmers, and crafts people. Their job was to make money through business and farming to support the two higher castes. They are also allowed to make sacrifices and study the Rig-Veda.

Sudra were made up of poor people and servants. There were many more people in this caste than in the others. Their only job was to serve the first three castes.

to build, and that was sad news to the people in slavery.

God showed Ezekiel that there would also be some changes in the way he wanted his people to worship him in the new temple. He didn't want them just to follow his rules with their hands. He wanted the people he loved to worship him with pure hearts. He wanted them to live according to his commands and to obey them out of love for him, just as he wants us to do today.

BIBLE MYSTERY
Where and how did Jeremiah the prophet die? *Answer: 575 B.C. One legend says Jeremiah was stoned to death in Egypt. Another legend says he was taken to Babylon, where he died. No one is certain how Jeremiah died or where, except God.*

Ezekiel's
Temple Vision

Nebuchadnezzar's
Insanity

Writing On
the Wall

572 B.C.

562 B.C.

542 B.C.

570 B.C.—Ahmose II
becomes king of Egypt.

570 B.C.—Cleitias, a Greek
vase painter of the Black
Figure style, is active.

561 B.C.—Peisistratus becomes
tyrant of Athens.

560 B.C.—Croesus succeeds
his father Alyattes as king
of Lydia.

550 B.C.—Cyrus the Great
conquers the Medes and
founds the Achaemenid
Persian empire.

543 B.C.—Colombo is
settled in Sri Lanka.

Nebuchadnezzar
562 B.C. Believes in God

Daniel 4

History & Politics

561 B.C. Greece. Peisistratos became the
tyrant ruler of the city of Athens.

*D*uring his years as king of Babylon,
Nebuchadnezzar had seen God's mighty
power at work several times. The first time was
when God helped Daniel tell the king his dream
and what it meant. (See "Daniel and the Dream"
on page 132). The second time was when
Shadrach, Meshach, and Abednego were saved
from the fiery furnace by an angel of God. (See
"Four Men in a Fire" on page 150).

Still, Nebuchadnezzar did not really believe
in God as the only God of heaven. He continued to
worship his other false gods, too... until something
really strange happened to him.

569-526 B.C. Egypt. King Amasis II was a great lover of music, drama, and the arts. He gave a lot of money to help develop them.

Religion, Philosophy & Learning

- 550 B.C. The first five books of the Bible, called the "Pentateuch," were clearly accepted as the Word of God or "Scriptures."
- 550 B.C. The Bible books of 1 Kings and 2 Kings were revised and finished.

The King's Dream

One night Nebuchadnezzar was sleeping when he had a scary dream. So he called for the wise men and fortune-tellers of Babylon to come and explain it to him. Just as before, Daniel was the only one who could explain its meaning.

The king's dream was about a tree that was so large it could be seen from all over the world. Then an angel told him to cut down the tree, cut off its branches, strip off its leaves, and scatter its fruit around. But he was supposed to leave the tree stump and its roots in the ground.

Daniel told Nebuchadnezzar that the tree in the dream stood for the king himself. And God had told him that what happened to the tree was going to hap-

BIBLE MYSTERY
What's the longest name in the Bible? *Answer: Did you say Nebuchadnezzar? Good guess, but it's really "Maher-shalal-hash-baz"! He was the son of the prophet Isaiah. See Isaiah 8:1.*

pen to the king. He would be forced away from people. He would live among the wild animals, and he would even think as an animal thinks. But when that time was over, God said that Nebuchadnezzar's kingdom would be given back to him.

"Now I, Nebuchadnezzar, give praise and honor and glory to the King of heaven. Everything he does is right. He is always fair. And he is able to make proud people humble."

Daniel 4:37

Music
Greece. The great musical Dionysia was given by Peisistratus in the city of Athens.

The Dream Came True

One day Nebuchadnezzar was walking around on his roof. He might have been

Science, Technology & Growth

- Rome. The Roman lunar year had ten months of varying lengths.
- 550 B.C. Pythagoras developed his math theorem that explained the size relationship of the sides of a right triangle.

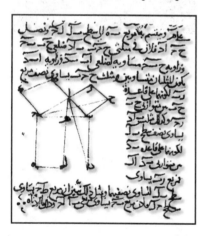

walking through the beautiful Hanging Gardens that he had built on his roof. He was thinking to himself how great a king he was and what wonderful things he had done as king. Then God spoke to him and told him that his dream was going to come true.

Right away, Nebuchadnezzar was forced away from people. He ate grass like an ox. His mind began thinking as an animal's does. His hair grew long like the feathers of an eagle. His fingernails grew long like the claws of a bird. And he stayed that way for seven years.

At last the time was over. The king looked up to heaven, and his thinking was right again. Then he praised God as the Most High God. He gave honor and glory to him. Then God gave the king back his kingdom, and he became even greater than before.

Nebuchadnezzar wrote a long letter telling everyone that God is the only

HISTORY MYSTERY

When did the people of Judah start being nicknamed "Jews"?

Answer: When they were captives in Babylon.

God to worship and serve. And he sent the letter to all the people in all the world. Finally, Nebuchadnezzar really believed in God!

DID YOU KNOW THAT...

the Bible is not
the only record
of King Nebuchadnezzar's
temporary insanity?
It is also reported
in the books of history
of Babylon.

Weapons of War

Nebuchadnezzar's army was powerful. The prophet Habakkuk said that their "armies march quickly like a whirlwind in the desert" (Habakkuk 1:9). Here are some of the ways the army of Babylon captured cities, including Jerusalem.

Fires. Sometimes they built fires at the base of the city walls. The heat from the fires caused the stones in the wall to crack. Then they would slowly wear away, and the army could break through the wall.

Catapults. Other times Babylonians used devices called catapults. These weapons shot huge boulders against the city walls, or over the walls into the city. Sometimes they even shot dead bodies with deadly diseases over the wall into the city. The diseases killed the people in the city.

Tunnels. Babylonians also tried to dig tunnels under the walls of the city so soldiers could sneak into the city and attack them from inside their own walls.

Battering rams. They also used huge logs to beat against the gates and walls of the city to knock them down.

Ramps. Often Babylonians built dirt ramps against the city walls. The ramps were like roads that went to the top of the city walls. Then the Babylonian army charged up the ramps, jumped over the walls, and attacked the city. This is how they captured Jerusalem.

Fighting back. People in the cities fought back against Babylon by shooting arrows, throwing rocks, and pouring hot oil from the wall down on the Babylonians below. But no cities could survive an attack by the mighty army of Babylon.

561 B.C.—Peisistratus becomes tyrant of Athens.

560 B.C.—Croesus succeeds his father Alyattes as king of Lydia.

550 B.C.—Lao-Tzu develops the Tao-te Ching, outlining the false philosophy of Taoism.

550 B.C.—The first plays are performed in Greece.

543 B.C.—Colombo is settled in Sri Lanka.

539 B.C.—The Persians under Cyrus the Great conquer Babylon.

542 B.C. The Finger of God

The Book of Job
Daniel 5

History & Politics

- 550 B.C. Persia. Cyrus the Great conquered the Medes and founded the Persian Empire.

- 547 B.C. Lydia. Cyrus the Great defeated King Croesus and captured the capital city of Sardis.

- China's rival states are combined under Shih Huang Ti—the first emporer of China.

King Nebuchadnezzar finally believed in God near the end of his reign. After he died, several other kings ruled over Babylon for short times. At last, King Belshazzar began to rule.

During this same time, the prophets Jeremiah and Ezekiel both died. And one of the kings of Babylon, named Evil-Merodach, released King Jehoiachin of Judah from prison and gave him back his place as an honored king. Meanwhile, Daniel continued to live and prophesy in Babylon.

Job

It might have also been during these years that the story of a man named Job was written. The Book of Job tells how a good man was tested by Satan and lost everything he had, including his family. But after Job went through much suffering, God gave him back more than he had had before his troubles began. The story may have been written to give hope to the people of Judah, who were still suffering in slavery in Babylon. Some of those people had stayed faithful to God, but they had to suffer anyway.

Belshazzar's Banquet

King Belshazzar was giving a large banquet. More than a 1,000 people were there! During the party, Belshazzar had the beautiful things taken from the Temple of God in Jerusalem brought to him. Then he and his guests drank wine from them. But they praised their own false gods, instead of the God of heaven.

HISTORY MYSTERY
Where did the saying "read the handwriting on the wall" come from?

Answer: It came from King Belshazzar's party where a hand wrote God's message of doom on the wall. Today, when people know something bad is probably going to happen, they might say, "You can read the handwriting on the wall."

Literature & Theater

550-460 B.C. Sicily. Epicharmus of Megara wrote some of the first comedy plays.

Religion, Philosophy & Learning

560-480 B.C. India. The religion of Buddha was founded by a young prince named Siddhartha Gautama.

Visual Arts

Asia Minor. The Temple of Artemis was built at Ephesus. This amazing temple was considered to be one of the Seven Wonders of the Ancient World.

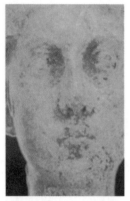

Science, Technology & Growth

546 B.C. Anaximander wrongly taught that all life comes from amphibians (water creatures).

Mind Meld

"Suddenly a person's hand appeared. The fingers wrote words on the plaster on the wall… in the royal palace. The king watched the hand as it wrote."

Daniel 5:5

Suddenly a person's hand wrote words on the wall of the royal palace. Belshazzar watched the hand as it wrote. And he was terrified! His face turned white with fear, and his knees knocked together. He couldn't even stand up because his legs were too weak.

Belshazzar called for the magicians and wise men to come and tell him what the strange words were and what they meant. But they could not read the words. Then Daniel was brought to the king.

Daniel said the words were these:

Mene, mene, tekel, parsin.

And he told the king that the words meant this: "*Mene*: God has counted the days until your kingdom will end. *Tekel*: You have been weighed on the scales and found not good enough. *Parsin*: Your kingdom is being divided between the Medes and the Persians."

Belshazzar rewarded Daniel with a royal robe, a gold chain, and he made him the third highest ruler in all of Babylon. But that night,

The Buddha

A young prince named Siddhartha Gautama was born about 563 B.C. near the mountains of Himalaya. Just before he became thirty years old, he was so moved when he saw suffering people, he left his father's palace, his wife, and his son and went away to find a better way of life.

He went to live in a forest as a "holy man." There he went without food and thought out a new, kinder religion than the Hindu religion he had always known. When he finished his thinking, he believed that the truth had been given to him. So he gave his first sermon to five men called "wisdom seekers," who had gone with him to the forest.

From then on, he was called "the Buddha," which means "the enlightened one." Sadly, he was worshiped instead of God. He taught that suffering is brought on by peoples' desires, and that suffering can be ended by ending all desires. Then, he said, happiness can be found.

Buddha taught people to be kind to all living things. And the people liked this gentle teaching that turned away from the cruel caste system. (See "The Caste System" on page 157.) Buddha wanted people to treat everyone—women and men, rich and poor—with kindness and respect. His teachings were in the everyday language of the people, too.

People listened to Buddha, instead of to God, and his ideas spread from India, where they began, to China and Japan. Today millions of people worship the false god called Buddha.

just as God had said through Daniel, Belshazzar was killed. He had worshiped false gods. He had not worshiped the God of heaven. And his kingdom was taken away from him.

Writing On the Wall	Daniel in the Lions' Den	Return to Jerusalem
542 B.C.	541 B.C.	538 B.C.

543 B.C.—Colombo is settled in Sri Lanka.

539 B.C.—The Persians under Cyrus the Great conquer Babylon.

537 B.C.—The Persians free the Jews from Babylonian rule.

541 B.C.

Daniel 6

God Saves Daniel from Lions

*W*ho killed Belshazzar? No one really knows for sure, but it might have been Darius the Mede. God had written on the wall that Belshazzar's kingdom would be divided between the Medes and the Persians. And Darius the Mede became ruler of Babylon when Belshazzar died.

A Plot Against Daniel

*D*arius liked Daniel and appointed him as one of three supervisors over Babylon. Before long, Daniel had done such a good job that Darius was planning to

History & Politics

- 543 B.C. Sri Lanka. The city of Colombo was settled.

- 578-534 B.C. Rome. Servius Tullius, who was King of Rome, set up the Class System based on how much property a person owned. This Class System would remind us of the Caste System in India. (See "The Caste System" on page 157.)

Sri Lanka

Literature & Theater

- Babylon. The Book of Daniel in the Bible was probably written.
- Greece. Public libraries were built in Athens.

Religion, Philosophy & Learning

550 B.C. China. Lao-tzu founded the false religion of Taoism. Tao means "the Way" to happiness. Lao-tzu believed people should lead simple and natural lives in harmony with nature. By understanding nature's way, he said people could achieve inner peace.

make Daniel ruler over all of Babylon. The other supervisors and governors didn't want Daniel to be promoted. So they tried to find something bad about Daniel to tell the king. But they couldn't find anything bad about Daniel. He was trustworthy. He was not lazy and didn't cheat the king. But finally, they thought of a plan.

The supervisors and governors went to see King Darius. They talked him into making a new law that no one could pray to any god except Darius for thirty days. If they did, they would be put into a den of lions. In those days, a law made by the king could not be changed—not even by the king himself.

Then King Darius said, "Daniel's God is the living God. He lives forever. His kingdom will never be destroyed. His rule will never end."

Daniel 6:26

Daniel Prayed Anyway

When Daniel heard about the new law, he went home, opened the window toward Jerusalem, and prayed to God, just as he had always done. He kept on doing this three times every day.

So the supervisors and governors went to King Darius and told him what

BIBLE MYSTERY

What wild animal is mentioned most often in the Bible?

Answer: The lion. It's mentioned about 130 times!

HISTORY MYSTERY

What other great discovery did Thales of Greece make?

Answer: Thales also knew that a magnet attracts iron, and that when amber was rubbed it became magnetic.

Visual Arts

Greece. The Temple of Apollo was built at Delphi, and the Temple of Zeus was built in Olympia.

Science, Technology & Growth

545 B.C. Greece. Thales of the city of Miletus developed "Thales' Proposition," which says that triangles over the diameter of a circle are right-angled. This is one of the oldest theories of mathematics.

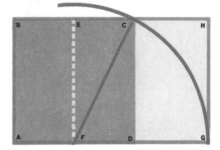

Daily Life

550-510 B.C. Greece. Travelers' maps were first drawn of large land areas by Anaximander.

Daniel was doing. They reminded Darius about the law he had made and said Daniel should be put into the lions' den. This upset Darius very much. He tried all day to think of a way to save Daniel, but his law couldn't be changed. So, that night, Daniel was put into a deep pit of hungry lions. Darius said to Daniel, "May the God you serve all the time save you!"

God's Angel

King Darius stayed up all night. He couldn't sleep because he was worried about Daniel. The next morning Darius went to the lions' den. He found Daniel alive and well. An angel of God had closed the mouths of the lions. Darius was very happy.

Then Darius had all the evil supervisors and governors thrown into the lions' den, and they were killed instantly. And he wrote a letter to everyone in Babylon telling them to worship the true God of heaven—the God of Daniel who had saved him.

It's a
FACT!

In spite of what he had seen and said, Darius the Mede did not continue to worship God. Stay tuned to see what happened to him!

Mapping the World

Until this time people only had maps of their own lands and estates. About 550 B.C. a man named Anaximander, a philosopher from the seaport city of Miletus in Greece, began drawing maps of large areas of the country for travelers. He engraved his maps on tablets of stone.

Anaximander drew the earth as round, with all the people living only on one side. He also made it appear that the earth was being watched from somewhere above it, as if by a bird or a god. No one had thought of doing this before; so many of the people who saw Anaximander's maps didn't like them.

The idea that the earth is round probably came to Anaximander because he was a student of the great philosopher, Thales. This teacher drew different shapes on tablets, such as straight lines, points, triangles, and circles. Then he and his students discussed used the drawings to talk about problems of measurements and relationships. This was the beginning of the study of Geometry. And Thales believed this new knowledge would help people better understand the universe.

The maps that Anaximander, Hecataeus, and other Greeks drew at this time remained the best maps until about A.D. 100-200. Then a man named Claudius Ptolemy improved on the Greek maps.

Today we have wonderful maps of almost anywhere in the world we want to go, thanks to Anaximander and the mapmakers who have lived after him.

Daniel in the
Lions' Den

Return to
Jerusalem

Haggai &
Zechariah

541 B.C.

538 B.C.

520 B.C.

539 B.C.—The Persians
under Cyrus the Great
conquer Babylon.

537 B.C.—The Persians
free the Jews from
Babylonian rule.

534 B.C.—Actor Thespis wins
first prize in a tragedy competition in Athens.
525 B.C.—The Persians under
Cambyses II conquer Egypt.

Judah Returns to Jerusalem!

538 B.C.

Ezra 1—2

History & Politics

- 539 B.C. Babylon. Cyrus the Great led the Persians to conquer Babylon.
- 530 B.C. Persia. Cyrus the Great was killed in battle.

The mighty empire of Babylon was growing weak and finally coming to an end. And Darius the Mede could see what was about to happen. But, instead of standing up for his people and being a man of honor, like Daniel was, Darius deserted Babylon. He became a traitor. He even helped Cyrus the Great, King of Persia, take over Babylon and become her king, too. After that, the Babylonians were never a powerful people again. And Babylonia became part of Persia.

The King's Announcement

Cyrus the Great was not like the kings of Babylon who had ruled the people of Judah (now called "Jews") before him. In his very first year as king

174

HISTORY MYSTERY
What kind of writing "paper" were Confucius' wise sayings probably written on in China?

Answer: Long pieces of silk. They used Chinese brushes and ground up a solid block of ink on a stone with a little water.

of Persia, he made an announcement to the Jews, who were still living there as slaves. He said that God had appointed him to rebuild the Temple in Jerusalem. And he announced that all the Jews were free to go back to Jerusalem to help build the Temple. They didn't have to go, but they could go if they wanted to. The Jews who stayed in Persia were told to help support the ones who would go to Jerusalem by giving them money, supplies, cattle, and special gifts for the Temple.

Getting Ready

When they heard the king's announcement, the family leaders of the tribes of Judah and Benjamin got ready to go to Jerusalem. So did the priests and the

Literature & Theater

- The Bible books of 1 Chronicles and 2 Chronicles were probably written.
- 551-479 B.C. China. The sayings of Confucius were collected into the famous work called *Analects*.

- 534 B.C. Greece. Playwright, Thespis, won first prize in a competition of sad plays (called "tragedies") in the city of Athens.

Religion, Philosophy & Learning

- 537 B.C. Persia. Cyrus the Great freed the Jews and allowed them to return to their homeland.

- 551-479 B.C. China. The Chinese philosopher, Confucius, lived and taught.

Visual Arts:

Gold treasures were found at Valci Tran. These showed the work of the Thracian people in the lower Danube area of the country.

Science, Technology & Growth

Greece. A Greek medical scientist named Alcmaeon from the city of Croton discovered the difference between veins and arteries in the human body. He also discovered how the brain and the organs of the senses (seeing, smelling, feeling, tasting, and hearing) work together.

Daily Life

Persia. The first coin was made that had a picture of the king on it.

Before this time coins had been made with pictures of animals. In Greece, coins had an owl on them. In Lydia, coins had a tortoise on them.

Levites. They were going to Jerusalem to build the Temple of the Lord. God made all these people want to go. And all their neighbors helped them. Cyrus also helped by giving the Jews back the beau-

Mind Meld

King Cyrus said, "The Lord… has appointed me to build a Temple for him at Jerusalem in Judah. Now all of you who are God's people are free to go to Jerusalem. May your God be with you."

Ezra 1:2-3

tiful things that had been taken out of the Temple in Jerusalem by King Nebuchadnezzar when Jerusalem was destroyed. There were 5,400 pieces of gold and silver! Sheshbazzar, the prince of Judah, brought all these things along when the captives went to Jerusalem.

The total number of Jews who returned to Jerusalem was 42,360. This didn't count their servants and singers. They also took many horses, mules, camels, and donkeys with them.

It's a FACT!

Before Jerusalem was destroyed, Jeremiah predicted that the Jews would be captives for seventy years. (See Jeremiah 25:11-12 and 29:10.) It was exactly seventy years when they went back to Jerusalem!

Who Was Confucius?

During the same time that the Jews were rebuilding the Temple in Jerusalem, a man named Confucius was having great influence on the people of China.

Confucius lived from 551 to 479 B.C. and became one of the most respected teachers and philosophers, not only in China, but in the world. He traveled all over China to teach people his way of thinking. He wanted to make China a better place to live by improving how people treated each other and how government worked. For instance, he believed that the emperor of China should be like a father to the people, and the people should love and obey him as children.

Here are some of the things that Confucius taught. He said these are guidelines to a happy and useful life.

Relationships: There are five relationships that need to be honored. They are ruler and subject, father and son, husband and wife, older brother and younger brother, friend and friend.

Attitudes: People should be sincere, polite, and unselfish.

Respect: People should obey and respect the laws and traditions of their country.

Work and Learn : People should work hard and respect learning.

Confucius said many wise things, which were written down by his followers in a collection called *Analects*. These people began to worship Confucius, but he was not the true God. He was a false god. Today more than 5.6 million people worship the false god Confucius.

BIBLE MYSTERY

Who never needs to sleep?

Answer: God. Psalm 121:3-4 says that God doesn't need to sleep. He is always awake and watching out for his people, just as he did for Judah.

Back Home

When the captives arrived at the site of the old Temple of the Lord, they made special offerings to help rebuild the Temple. They gave as much as they could. The Temple would be built again in the same place it had been before.

All the Jews settled in their hometowns. They were finally back home in the Promised Land, just as God had said they would be so long ago.

Return to Jerusalem	Haggai & Zechariah	New Temple Completed
538 B.C.	520 B.C.	516 B.C.

537 B.C.—The Persians free the Jews from Babylonian rule.
534 B.C.—Actor Thespis wins first prize in a tragedy competition in Athens.

520 B.C.—Epictetus, a Red Figure style painter of Greek vases, is active.

518 B.C.—Darius I begins building the city of Persepolis as the Persian royal residence.

520 B.C.

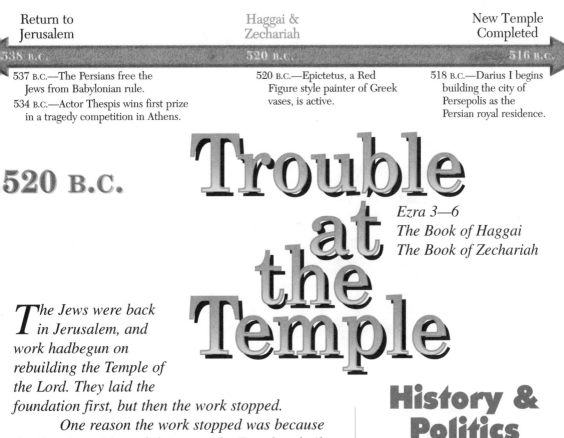

Trouble at the Temple

Ezra 3—6
The Book of Haggai
The Book of Zechariah

The Jews were back in Jerusalem, and work hadbegun on rebuilding the Temple of the Lord. They laid the foundation first, but then the work stopped.

One reason the work stopped was because the Jews' neighbors didn't want the Temple rebuilt. So they tried to stop the project. Another reason the work stopped was because the Jews were busy getting resettled in the land. King Nebuchadnezzar's armies had ruined Judah. The fields were full of weeds. The houses had been burned down. And the city buildings were all destroyed.

So the Jews had to work very hard rebuilding their own houses, planting crops, and repairing the destruction of the whole country of Judah. They didn't think they had time to work on the Temple of the Lord. They thought they would work on the Temple when everything else had been finished. But that was not what God wanted them to do.

History & Politics

522 B.C. Judah. Zerubbabel was appointed governor of Judah. He and the Jews' high priest, Joshua, led a large group of Jews out of exile in Babylon and back to Jerusalem.

Literature and Theater

- 525–456 B.C. Greece. Aeschylus, a famous Greek dramatist, lived and wrote. He wrote over ninety plays, including *Oresteia* and the famous *Prometheus Bound*.

- Judah. The Bible books of Haggai and Zechariah were probably written.

Religion, Philosophy & Learning

- 520 B.C. Judah. The foundation of the new Temple of God was laid.
- Jerusalem is still in ruins. The people are deeply discouraged.

JERUSALEM

God's Reminder

God sent two prophets to the Jews to remind them about the importance of building the Temple. These two prophets were named Haggai and Zechariah. Haggai preached sermons that reminded the people that building the Temple was more important than anything else they had to do. He told them to finish the Temple first, and then tend to their own houses and lands. He said that the reason they were having so much trouble was because they had made their own houses and lands more important than the house (Temple) of God.

Zechariah's messages were different than Haggai's. God sent Zechariah eight special dreams that gave the Jews hope for the future. Zechariah's message of hope was important because the Jews would have

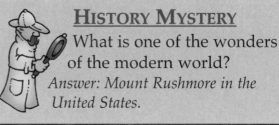

HISTORY MYSTERY
What is one of the wonders of the modern world?
Answer: Mount Rushmore in the United States.

to wait hundreds of years before God acted again. Zechariah warned the Jews about the long wait they would have. And he told them about what would happen during those long years of waiting.

Work Is Begun Again

The leaders and people of Judah listened to Haggai and Zechariah, and they began working on the Temple right away. Then Haggai gave them a special promise from God. Because the Jews had

DID YOU KNOW THAT...

Zechariah placed a crown on Joshua, the high priest. This was a symbol that meant Jesus would someday be both high priest and king over his people. From that time on, the high priest was more like a king to the Jews.

Music

520–447 B.C. Greece. Pindar, a great composer and poet, lived and worked.

The Seven Wonders of the Ancient World

The Seven Wonders of the Ancient World are buildings and statues from ancient times that were amazing to the people of that time. This list of wonders was made over 2,000 years ago by a Greek writer. Today, all of these wonders have been destroyed or have crumbled away, except the pyramids of Egypt. Here are the seven wonders:

The Statue of Zeus. This beautiful statue of the false god Zeus was made of marble, gold, and ivory. It was in the city of Olympia in Greece.

The Hanging Gardens. King Nebuchadnezzar II built wonderful gardens and terraces on the roof of his palace in Babylon. Water had to be pumped to these gardens.

The Mausoleum. This building is a monument and tomb for a king in Asia Minor named Mausolus. His wife built it for him when he died. It was located at Halicarnassus.

God said to Judah, "You are busy working on your own houses. But my house is still in ruins!"

Haggai 1:9

listened to the two prophets and obeyed the Lord, he promised to bless them. And he did bless the Jews who were faithful to him during this time.

Zechariah's messages from God were important for two reasons. First, they gave the Jews hope for the future. Second, they showed that God's plan from the very beginning of time had not changed. He was still planning to send his Son Jesus into the world. And it was Jesus who would walk through this very Temple that the Jews were building. It was Jesus who would fill the Temple they were building with the glory of God himself. It was Jesus who would save the Jews and all of God's people in the world from their sins. God would send Jesus into the world because he loved his people so much.

The Colossus of Rhodes. The Greeks built an enormous statue of their false god Helios in the harbor of the city of Rhodes. It was later destroyed by an earthquake.

The Temple of Artemis. This temple was built by the Greeks to their false goddess, Artemis. The temple was in the city of Ephesus. An army that attacked Ephesus burned this temple to the ground later.

The Pharos Lighthouse. This was a huge lighthouse in Egypt.

The Great Pyramids of Egypt. Still standing today, the pyramids were the amazing tombs for the kings of Egypt (pharaohs). You can still see them and climb them if you go to Egypt.

BIBLE MYSTERY

What does the Bible compare to a scarecrow?

Answer: False gods. The prophet Jeremiah said idols were like scarecrows because they can't speak or walk. See Jeremiah 10:5.

520 B.C.—Epictetus, a Red Figure style painter of Greek vases, is active.

512 B.C.—Darius I conquers the city of Byzantium.

480 B.C.—The Persians defeat the Greeks at Thermopylae; Athens is burned.

516 B.C.

Ezra 6
The Book of Zechariah

The New Temple Is Finished

History & Politics

- 507 B.C. Greece. The form of government known as democracy was first set up in the city of Athens.
- 509 B.C. Rome. The people of Rome set up a republic form of government.

*O*n March 12, 516 B.C., the new Temple of the Lord in Jerusalem was finished. This was in the sixth year that Darius was king of Persia. The Jews were successful because they listened to the messages from God that came to them through Haggai and Zechariah. And they obeyed God's words.

Celebration!

Then the people of God celebrated. They gave the Temple to God to honor him. Everybody was happy! The Priests, the Levites, and the rest of the Jews who had come back from slavery were excited. They weren't slaves anymore. They had their Promised Land back. They had their homes and families

184

HISTORY MYSTERY
On what day was Julius Caesar, the King of Rome, murdered?
Answer: On the Ides of March. "Ides" means "middle." So he was murdered on March 15, 44 B.C.

back together. And God had kept his promises.

This is how they gave the Temple to God. They offered these sacrifices to him: 100 bulls, 200 male sheep, and 400 male lambs. And as an offering to forgive the sins of all the nation of Israel, they offered 12 male goats—one for each of the 12 tribes of Israel. Then they put the priests and Levites into their separate groups. Each group had a certain time to serve God in the Temple at Jerusalem. This was all done just as it was commanded in the Book of Moses.

The Passover

Then the Jews who had returned from slavery in Babylon celebrated the Passover feast. They celebrated it just as the people of Israel had done when God led them out of slavery in Egypt so many

Literature & Theater

- 500 B.C. Greece. Pindar, a famous Greek poet, began to write his odes, which are poems that are written to be sung.
- 520 B.C. Greece. The well-known poet, Anacreon, became the official poet of the Greek courts.

Religion, Philosophy & Learning

516 B.C. Judah. The new Temple of the Lord was finished in Jerusalem.

Visual Arts

515 B.C. Persia. King Darius built a splendid capital at the city of Persepolis.

185

582–497 B.C. Greece. The philosopher, Pythagoras, used math to define pitches of the scale of notes. From this the Greeks began to write music, using letters of the alphabet to stand for the different musical pitches. We still use this system today.

Science, Technology & Growth

- 500 B.C. Persia. King Darius had a 125-mile-long canal dug between the Nile River and the Gulf of Suez. This made ship travel possible between the Mediterranean Sea and the Red Sea for the first time.
- 500 B.C. India. The first eye surgeries for cataracts were performed.

years before. The priests and Levites made themselves clean, as God's law commanded. So they killed the Passover lambs for all the Jews who had returned from slavery, for their relatives, the priests, and for themselves.

So all the Jews who had come back from slavery ate the Passover lamb. So did those who had given up the unclean ways they had learned from non-Jewish neighbors. They worshiped the Lord, the God of Israel, the God of the Jews.

This was the greatest celebration the Jews had enjoyed in decades. And it

"They finished building the Temple as the God of Israel had said... Then the people of Israel celebrated."

Ezra 6:14, 16

went on for seven days! The Lord had made them happy. And they continued to praise him for the wonderful things he had done for them.

Last Words of Zechariah

After that, Zechariah gave his last messages from God to the Jews. Although it was still hundreds of years before Jesus would be born, God showed Zechariah important details about Jesus. So he tells the Jews that when Jesus comes, he will not be like the kings they've had in the past. He will not be a king of war, but he

DID YOU KNOW THAT...

there were two kings
of Persia
named "Darius"?
And there were two kings
of Persia
named "Xerxes."

Daily Life

500 B.C. China. Carpet was first made in Chinese and/or Persian workshops.

The City of Rome

About 750 B.C., some small villages were built in an area of seven hills on the Tiber River far away in southern Europe. Those small villages grew bigger until they later became one large town called Rome. It was often called "The City of the Seven Hills." Many years later Rome became the largest empire in the world. By the time Jesus came, the city of Rome had over a million people living in it.

Republic. The people of Rome got rid of their king and set up a new form of government called a republic. In a republic there is no king, and the people choose (vote for) the people they want to run the government. Only "free men" (men who were not slaves) were allowed to vote; women and slaves could not vote.

Classes. In Rome, the people were divided into two groups or "classes." The patricians were rich, important people. The plebeians were less wealthy people, such as farmers and workers. In the early years of the republic, the patricians controlled the government. Only patricians could be in the Senate where the laws were made. So the laws were often unfair to the plebeians, who could not go to the Senate.

Rulers. Two famous rulers of the Roman Empire were Julius Caesar and his son, Augustus. Julius Caesar made life better for the plebeians; so he became their hero. But he was murdered by some patricians. Then Augustus became ruler and brought many years of peace and progress to Rome. Augustus was ruling Rome when Jesus was born.

will be a king of peace. He will not come in riding in a chariot, but he will come riding a gentle donkey. He will be a loving king of the heart, just as God had always been to the Jews.

BIBLE MYSTERY

How were some birds used like calendars by the Jews?

Answer: The Jews knew that some birds migrated at exactly the same time every year. This was especially true of the storks that migrated along the Jordan River Valley in spring. See Jeremiah 8:7.

188

New Temple Completed	Esther and Mordecai	Malachi's Prophecy
516 B.C.	480 B.C.	465 B.C.

512 B.C.—Darius I conquers the city of Byzantium.

480 B.C.—Siddhartha Guatama, the false god, Buddha, dies in India.
480 B.C.—Greek philosopher, Pythagoras of Samos dies.

478 B.C.—The Delian League is established under the leadership of Athens.

465 B.C.—Xerxes is assassinated; his son Artaxerxes I succeeds him as king of Persia.

480 B.C. Queen Esther Saves God's People

The Book of Esther

About forty years had passed since the new Temple in Jerusalem had been finished. The Jews were still working to restore their country to what it had been before Babylon had ruined it. King Darius had died about three years before this chapter in the story of God's people happened. And a new King of Persia named Xerxes (ZERK-cees) was ruling.

The Party

King Xerxes gave a huge banquet for all the important people in the whole Persian Empire. The banquet lasted 180 days! During the party Xerxes showed off all the wealth of his kingdom and the splendor of his own kingship. One of the things he wanted to show off was his queen. So he sent for Queen Vashti to

History & Politics

- 480 B.C. Persia. The Persian Wars began. The Greeks were defeated at Thermopylae.
- 490 B.C. Greece. The Persian army was defeated by the Greeks on the Plain of Marathon.
- 490 B.C. Africa. Hanno of the city of Carthage led an expedition of sixty ships down the west coast of Africa as far as Gambia. There they set up six cities.

189

Literature & Theater

- 520–421 B.C. Greece. Cratinus, Greek author of funny plays (called "comedies") lived and wrote.

- Persia. The Bible book of Esther was probably written.

Religion, Philosophy & Learning

- Greece. Great thinkers, Socrates and Plato, began the study of philosophy in Athens. Philosophy is still studied today.

- Greece. The rules of geometry were invented by Euclid and Pythagoras. These are still used today.

Did you know that...

the Book of Esther
is the only book
in the Bible
that does not actually
mention the name of God.

come to the banquet wearing her royal crown. But she would not go. (The reason Queen Vashti would not go to the king's party was because he might have been asking her to come wearing only the royal crown… and no clothes!) This made Xerxes angry; so he took Vashti off the throne, and she was no longer queen.

The Contest

Then all the pretty young women from all over Persia were brought to Xerxes so he could choose a new queen. He finally chose a beautiful young Jewish girl named Esther. And the king loved her very much.

The Plot

An important man named Haman hated the Jewish people. That was because Esther's uncle Mordecai would not bow down to Haman as he passed him on the street. So Haman tricked Xerxes into signing a law saying the Persians could kill all the Jews in the Persian Empire on a certain day. (Haman didn't know that Queen Esther was Mordecai's niece and a Jew.)

BIBLE MYSTERY
Which Bible queen had a "heavenly" name?
Answer: Esther. Her name means "star."

- China. The Buddha, Siddhartha Gautama, died.

Visual Arts

Greece. The Greeks began using columns (supports) with decorated tops (called "capitals") to hold up the roofs of their temples. The three kinds of capitals were called Doric, Ionic, and Corinthian. You may be able to spot these column styles on present-day buildings.

Music

500 B.C. Greece. Choral music was at its best.

Science, Technology & Growth

- Greece. Aristotle, the famous philosopher, studied scientific problems in the areas of metaphysics, physics, astronomy, meteorology, and biology.
- 500 B.C. The brain was identified as the center of human intelligence.
- 480 B.C. Persia. The first pontoon bridge (or floating bridge) was invented. Armies used these to cross rivers.

The Great Marathon Race

The Persian Empire was capturing countries and peoples all around. One of the greatest battles fought was between Persia and Greece on the Plain of Marathon in 490 B.C., just ten years after Esther saved God's people. Although the Persian armies were much stronger, Greece won this battle.

When it was over, a Greek messenger named Pheidippides ran about twenty-five

miles from Marathon to Athens to announce the great victory. As soon as he had made the announcement, Pheidippides dropped dead from being so tired.

Today, the famous Marathon Race is held each year in honor of Pheidippides and the great run he made. It's the longest race held in track-and-field contests. The longer length of the modern race (twenty-six miles) was set in A.D. 1908 at the London Olympics. It's the distance from Windsor Castle to the Olympic stadium.

Mordecai said to Esther, "Who knows, you may have been chosen queen for just such a time as this."

Esther 4:14

When Mordecai heard about the law, he sent a message to Esther, telling her to talk to King Xerxes and save the Jews. But the king had a law that no one was allowed to talk to him unless he called for them—not even the Queen. Anyone who disobeyed this law could be killed.

From 1896–1984 only men ran the marathon at the Olympics. Now, both men and women run the race. But there are no records for the marathon because each marathon race course is different. The best men's times are under two hours and seven minutes. The best women's times are slightly above two hours and twenty minutes.

Well-known marathon races today, like the ones held in New York and Boston, have thousands of runners in them, as well as thousands more watchers. A runner has to train for many months to run the marathon race... without dropping dead like Pheidippides!

The Rescue

Queen Esther was very brave. So she went to see the king anyway. She said, "If I die, then I die." But because he loved her, Xerxes did not kill her. Instead, he offered to give her anything she wanted, up to half his whole kingdom! When Esther told him about Haman's plot to kill her people, Xerxes became very angry. So he made another law that said the Jews could fight back if the Persians attacked them. Then he had Haman hanged on the very gallows Haman built for Esther's uncle Mordecai.

Brave Queen Esther had saved God's people from being destroyed. And every year after that, even up to today, the Jews have remembered the brave thing she did and how God rescued them by celebrating the Feast of Purim. It was a great day for the people of God.

BIBLE MYSTERY
How long did a young woman have to prepare herself before she was allowed to go in to the King of Persia?
Answer: At least a year!

Esther and Mordecai	Malachi's Prophecy	Nehemiah Rebuilds the Wall
480 B.C.	465 B.C.	444 B.C.

480 B.C.—Greek Philosopher, Heraclitus of Ephesus is active.

480 B.C.—The Greeks defeat the Persian navy at Salamisl; over 1,000 triremes are used.

472 B.C.—Aeschylus' earliest preserved play, *The Persians,* is performed.

460 B.C.—Pericles becomes the political leader of Athens.

447 B.C.—Building of the Parthenon begins in Athens.

465 B.C.

History & Politics

450 B.C. Rome. The law code called the Twelve Tables was written and put into use.

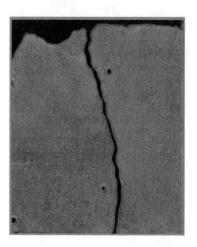

Malachi: Prophet of Hope

The Book of Malachi

A lmost twenty years passed after Esther saved God's people from being killed by the Persians. During that time King Xerxes' kingdom was failing. He was running out of money. And, finally, in 465 B.C. King Xerxes was murdered in his own bedroom in the palace. After that, his younger son became king. He was called Artaxerxes I.

Tired of Waiting

Meanwhile, the Jews had continued to rebuild their country and the Holy City of Jerusalem. They were trying to make it as wonderful as it had

194

once been. But they were getting tired of waiting for God to keep his promises about Jesus coming. They were tired of being ruled by Persia. They were starting to wonder again if God really cared about them or loved them. They had forgotten that the prophets Daniel and Zechariah had told them it would be a long wait.

The Jews had begun to wander away from God again, too. They had quit giving enough money to the Temple treasury to take care of the priests and Levites while they did their work. They had been offering sacrifices that were not pure. And the men had begun marrying women from foreign countries who

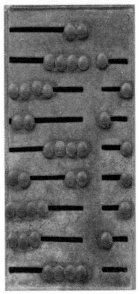
BIBLE MYSTERY

What does the word "Bible" mean?

Answer: It means "books." The Bible is a collection of sixty-six different books and letters. The first thirty-nine books are called the Old Testament. The last twenty-seven books are called the New Testament. Malachi is the last book of the Old Testament.

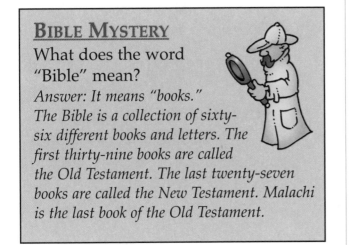

worshiped false gods. So God was not happy with them.

Malachi's Message

Then God answered their questions and told them how sad he was about the way they had been living. He sent a prophet named Malachi to bring the Jews a message from him. And the very first thing God said through Malachi was "I love you." In spite of everything the Jews had done wrong, God still loved them. They were his people, and they still had a special job to do because Jesus had not come yet.

Visual Arts

457 B.C. Greece. The Golden Age of art and architecture began.

Science, Technology & Growth

460–370 B.C. Greece. Hippocrates, the Father of Modern Medicine, lived and taught.

God said to Israel, "For you who honor me, goodness will shine on you like the sun. There will be healing in its rays."

Malachi 4:2

Day of the Lord's Judging

Malachi also told the people that a day would come when God would judge the people for the wrongs they had done. He said, "There is a day coming that will be like a hot furnace. All the proud and evil people will be like straw. On that day they will be completely burned up. But for you who honor me, goodness will shine on you like the sun. Then you will crush the wicked."

God was saying, "Don't give up, Israel! Hold on! The Messiah is still coming. I love you, and I will not forget my promises to you. Just be patient and wait a little longer."

Malachi's name told people what his job was. It means "messenger."

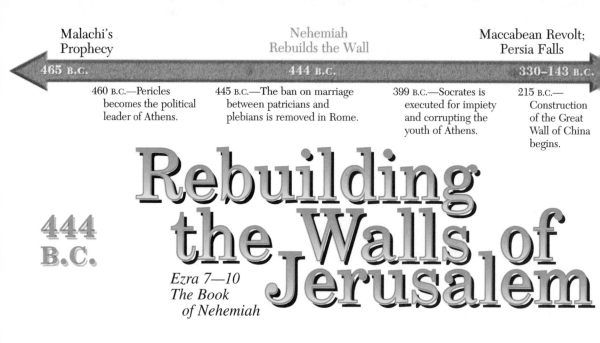

Malachi's
Prophecy

Nehemiah
Rebuilds the Wall

Maccabean Revolt;
Persia Falls

465 B.C.

444 B.C.

330–143 B.C.

460 B.C.—Pericles
becomes the political
leader of Athens.

445 B.C.—The ban on marriage
between patricians and
plebians is removed in Rome.

399 B.C.—Socrates is
executed for impiety
and corrupting the
youth of Athens.

215 B.C.—
Construction
of the Great
Wall of China
begins.

Rebuilding the Walls of Jerusalem

444 B.C.

Ezra 7—10
The Book
of Nehemiah

History & Politics

431–404 B.C. Greece. The Peloponnesian War raged between Sparta and Athens. Finally, Athens surrendered to Sparta. And a group of cruel rulers called The Thirty Tyrants were put into office.

*T*he Jews in Jerusalem had a long, hard task of rebuilding the Temple and the Holy City. The work was stopped many times by Israel's neighbors and enemies who didn't want Israel to become strong again. King Artaxerxes of Persia still supported them as they worked.

About 458 B.C. the great prophet and teacher of God's law named Ezra took fifteen hundred more Jews from Babylon back to Jerusalem to help with the rebuilding. It took them about five months to make the trip. But they took with them more treasures for the temple and the work of rebuilding.

When they arrived in Jerusalem, Ezra was sad to find that many men of Israel had married foreign wives. These women didn't believe in God, and they worshiped false gods. So Ezra told the men of Israel to divorce those foreign wives so they wouldn't begin following false gods, too. Many of them did as Ezra told them to do.

198

Nehemiah's Sadness

Back in the palace of King Artaxerxes in Babylon, about fourteen years after Ezra went to Jerusalem, news came to Nehemiah that Jerusalem's walls were broken down and her gates had been burned. Nehemiah was the king's cup-bearer. (He protected the king by tasting anything served to the king before the king ate or drank it. He did this so that no one could poison the king.) The news made Nehemiah very sad. He cried for several days. And he prayed.

When the king saw how sad Nehemiah was, he appointed him gover-nor over Jerusalem. And he sent

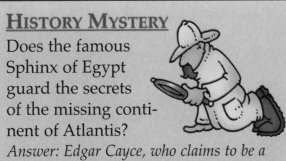

HISTORY MYSTERY

Does the famous Sphinx of Egypt guard the secrets of the missing conti-nent of Atlantis?

Answer: Edgar Cayce, who claims to be a modern-day prophet, thinks so. He says that the secret of where Atlantis was located was hidden in a small tomb or secret vault that's somewhere between the right paw of the Great Sphinx and the nearby River Nile. Is he right? No one knows because the vault has never been found.

Literature & Theater

- Judah. The Bible books of Nehemiah and Ezra were probably written.
- 498–406 B.C. Greece. Sophocles was a leading playwright, who wrote *Oedipus Rex*. He also invented a writing style called the dramatic form.
- 441–406 B.C. Greece. Euripedes was also a great playwright in Athens, who wrote *The Trojan Woman* and ninety-one other plays.
- 427–385 B.C. Greece. Aristophanes was the leading comic playwright in Athens, who wrote *Lysistrata*.

Religion, Philosophy & Learning

- 444 B.C. Judah. The walls of Jerusalem were rebuilt under the leadership of Nehemiah.
- 399 B.C. Greece. The famous philoso-pher, Socrates, was killed for teaching the young people of Athens to do wrong things.

Visual Arts

447–432 B.C. Greece. The amazing Parthenon temple to the false goddess Athena was built in Athens.

Music

400 B.C. Greece. The musical instrument called the aulos was in use. The aulos made musical sound by air being blown across a wooden reed, like a clarinet or saxophone today.

Science, Technology & Growth

- 437 B.C. Sri Lanka. A hospital, possibly the first one ever, was built.
- 400 B.C. Greece. The catapult, a great weapon of war, was invented. (See "Weapons of War" on page 163)
- 400 B.C. The disease of Malaria was identified. *Malaria* means "bad or poisonous air" (mal = "bad" and aria = "air"). People first thought the disease came from the bad air found in swamps and marshes. Later, it was found that Malaria is caused by the bite of a certain kind of mosquito. A person with Malaria usually has very high fever and chills.

Nehemiah to rebuild the walls and gates of the Holy City. When Nehemiah arrived in Jerusalem, he examined the wall to see what had to be done. Then he put the people of Judah to work on the wall.

Some of the workers rebuilt the city gates, while others worked on the wall. When they were attacked by their enemies, Nehemiah took half of the workers to guard the other half while they worked. And the Lord protected them.

Wall Finished

In only fifty-two days, the wall of Jerusalem was completely rebuilt, and all the gates were hung. Israel's enemies were shamed, and God's people were honored. Then Nehemiah led the people as they gave the walls and the gates to God, to honor him. After

"So the wall of Jerusalem was completed... Then all our enemies... understood that the work had been done with the help of our God."

Nehemiah 6:15–16

that, Ezra read the Law of God to all the people of Israel, and the people made a new promise to worship God and only him.

The Holy City and her mighty wall were rebuilt. And the Jews once again worshiped and praised the God who loved and cared for them. It was one of the greatest days in the history of God's people. What a wonderful way for the Old Testament to end!

But still a greater day was coming, both for the Jews and for all the world!

DID YOU KNOW THAT...

there are almost 400 years between the end of the Old Testament and the beginning of the New Testament? That's why the next section of this book is called "Between the Testaments."

BIBLE MYSTERY
What is another name for the Law of Moses that Ezra read to the people after the walls of Jerusalem were rebuilt?
Answer: The Torah.

Atlantis: The Lost Continent

During the period of time between the testaments of the Bible, beginning about 387 B.C., a Greek philosopher named Plato was writing about a place called Atlantis. Atlantis was supposed to have been a lost continent or a huge island where a highly developed people lived. According to those who studied it, Atlantis may have been destroyed by a great disaster of nature, such as The Flood, a volcano, or an earthquake. More than 2,000 books have been written about Atlantis!

Plato and his Greek friends believed the lost continent of Atlantis once existed west of Gibraltar. They thought it was swallowed up by the sea. Even 1,500 years later, in the Middle Ages, mapmakers were still marking the position of Atlantis on their maps. Even so, no one really knows where Atlantis was, if it existed at all.

Scholars today who believe that Atlantis was real don't agree on where it was located. They say it might have been in the Aegean Sea, or near the island of Bimini in the Bahamas. Some people of old thought Christopher Columbus had discovered Atlantis when he landed in the Americas. Other explorers believed that Atlantis was Azores in the middle of the Atlantic Ocean, or the Canary Islands. And others thought it was somewhere else.

People today may think that the idea of a lost continent is silly, but many serious researchers have taken time to look for it. Whether Atlantis was truth or fiction, its name lives on today as the Atlantic Ocean—the ocean that supposedly covered the mysterious missing land.

BETWEEN THE TESTAMENTS

425 B.C.—Sophocles' play **Oedipus Rex** is completed.	404 B.C.—Sparta conquers Athens and takes leadership of all Greece.	280 B.C.—The Pharos lighthouse, one of the Seven Wonders of the World, is built at Alexandria.	139 B.C.—The Romans defeat the Celts in the Iberian Peninsula and found Lusitania.	100 B.C.—Shadow puppets develop in China.

330–143 B.C.

From Old to New

*T*he Bible does not record what happens to the Jews during the next 400 years. Does that mean that nothing happened? Not at all! In fact, the time between the Old Testament record and the New Testament record was full of change for the Jews—social change, political change, language change, and even religious change.

Does the Bible's silence mean that God forgot about his people during that time? Not at all! In truth, the things that happened show that God was right there with his people as he had always been. He was getting the world ready for Jesus' birth, which comes right after this period of history ends.

History & Politics

- 390 B.C. Rome. The people of Gaul attacked Rome. The Romans quickly rebuilt their city and surrounded it with a wall.

- 300 B.C. France. A small fishing village was founded and named "Paris."

- 301–198 B.C. Palestine (Judah). Ptolemy of Egypt recaptured the land of the Jews, now called

203

"Palestine." They remained under Egypt's rule for a hundred years.

- 174 B.C. Palestine. The city of Jerusalem was renamed Antioch at Jerusalem. It was also given a Greek city government and a school called a gymnasion.
- 164 B.C. Palestine. The Feast of Hanukkah was first celebrated by the Jews in December as part of presenting the new Temple to God. This holiday ("holy day") is still celebrated by the Jewish people today.

Literature & Theater

- 375 B.C. Palestine. The Aramaic language was replacing Hebrew as the language of most Jews.
- 350 B.C. Palestine. The books of the prophets in the Bible were accepted as God's Word by the Jews, but they were not accepted by the Samaritan people.
- 300–200 B.C. Palestine. The Bible book of Psalms was probably completed.
- 294 B.C. Greece. The famous library and museum at Alexandria was built.

The Apocrypha

Does the Bible's silence mean that nothing was written about the Jews during that time? Not at all. There are fourteen books of history that tell us what happened to the Jews and other nations. These books are called The Apocrypha.

So, why are the books of The Apocrypha not in the Bible? The Jewish priests and Levites who decided which books about the Jews were from God did not believe that the books of The Apocrypha were from him. Some of these books even praised false gods and demons. So these books have never been included in the Hebrew (Jewish) Bible.

Does that mean that they are wrong about history? Not really. We can learn many true things about the history of the Jewish people during these years from the books of The Apocrypha, but we should remember that God probably did not write these books as he did the ones that are in the Bible.

Alexander the Great

From The Apocrypha we learn that during this 400-year period of time the Persian Empire grew weak and was defeated by the Greeks. Their leader was Alexander the Great, who was one of the greatest military leaders the world has ever known. He conquered so many lands that the East and West finally came together. And everywhere that Alexander's armies went, they took their language with them. It was called koine Greek. This was the language later used in the New Testament and while Jesus lived. God was putting it into place all over the world so that the Good News about Jesus could travel quickly.

The Septuagint

After Alexander died, two of his generals fought over and divided the lands he had conquered. And the Jews were caught between them. When some of the Jews were taken to the city of Alexandria in Egypt, something important happened. The Jewish scholars worked with Greek scholars to make a copy of the Law of Moses in the Greek language. In our Bible this would be the first five books of the Old Testament. This Greek copy was called the Septuagint. From then on, the Septuagint was used much more than the Hebrew copy by Jews who spoke Greek.

- 250 B.C. Egypt. The Law of Moses was put into the Greek language called the Septuagint. It became the Bible of Jews who spoke Greek and early Christians.
  - 250 B.C. Asia Minor. Parchment was developed as a type of writing material in Pergamum. It was made from animal skins. The skins were scraped, cleaned with lime to remove fat, and then stretched on a frame and left to dry. Parchment lasted longer than the papyrus people had been using for so many years.
- 240 B.C. Rome. Livius Andronicus produced the first Latin literature.

Religion, Philosophy & Learning

- 397–347 B.C. Greece. The great philosopher, Plato, was living and working in Athens. He founded the Academy, where his ideas were taught. He also wrote a work called *The Republic*.

- 322 B.C. Greece. The famous philosopher, Aristotle, died.

Visual Arts

- 370–330 B.C. Greece. Sculptors, Praxiteles and Scopas, were working in Athens.
- 333 B.C. Samaria. The Samaritan people built a temple to God on Mt. Gerizim near Shechem.
- 320 B.C. Greece. The first true portrait was painted of Aristotle.

Music

246–221 B.C. Egypt. Ctesibius of Alexandria invented the Hydraulis, which was a water-powered organ. It contained a set of pipes mounted on a chest. Air was forced into the chest by water pressure. To open and close the pipes, the organist pushed sliders that had holes in them into and out of the chest.

The Maccabees

One of the generals that took part of Alexander's lands was named Epiphanes. He was one of the meanest rulers to ever live. He ruled over the people called the Seleucids. He was cruel to the Jews. And he did some horrible things to them. The worst thing he did was to sacrifice a pig (a filthy animal that Jews were not allowed to own or touch under the Law of Moses) on an altar to his false god he had built in the very Temple of the Lord.

When that happened, a group of Jews called Maccabeans began attacking

It's a FACT!

The word "Septuagint" means "seventy." It was called this because it's believed that seventy scholars helped to translate the Law of Moses into Greek.

the Seleucids. They were led by a man named Mattathias. After twenty years of attacks, the Maccabeans got some help from a group of people called the Hasidim, and they won their freedom from the Seleucids in order to live under the rule of the Romans.

The Romans allowed the Jews to rule themselves for a few years, but the Jews knew that it would not last too long. So they continued to hope and look for Jesus, the Messiah, to come. They thought Jesus would be a great military leader, who would help them defeat the Romans. Then they thought he would set up a great kingdom that would last forever, just as God had promised them.

Science, Technology & Growth

- Greece. The scientist, Archimedes, designed the great water screw, which lifted water from one level to another. This invention is still in use today.
- 312 B.C. Rome. The famous road called the Appian Way was begun.
- 292–280 B.C. Rhodes. The Colossus of Rhodes was built in Rhodes Harbor. It's one of the Seven Wonders of the Ancient World (see page 182). The huge statue was over one hundred feet tall and made completely of bronze. It was destroyed by an earthquake in 224 B.C.
- 285 B.C. Egypt. The first known lighthouse was built at Pharos. It was one of the Seven Wonders of the Ancient World (see page 182).
- 260 B.C. India. Emperor Asoka planted herb gardens for medical use.
- 240 B.C. Greece. Eratosthenes, a famous geographer, calculated the size of the earth. He came within 10–15 percent of modern measurements.
- 239 B.C. Halley's comet was seen and recorded for the first time.
- 221 B.C. China. Gunpowder was invented.
- 200 B.C. Rome. Iron horseshoes were first developed.
- 200 B.C. China. Stirrups on saddles for horses were probably in use.
- 150 B.C. Rhodes. Hipparchus put together the first catalog of the stars.

They did not understand that Jesus would be a gentle leader who would teach them how to live in peace, no matter who was their earthly ruler. His kingdom would last forever, but it would not be an earthly kingdom. It would be a kingdom of the heart.

Daily Life

- 300 B.C. Rome. Cookies were first made. Did you ever think of Jesus eating cookies as a boy? He probably did, because Romans ruled the land where he grew up.
- 300 B.C. Rome. Ketchup was first made. Perhaps people in those days ate ketchup on their sheep burgers!
- 264 B.C. Rome. Gladiator fights were begun. Slaves fought to the death to entertain wealthy and important Romans.
- 200 B.C. Rome. The game of pitching horseshoes probably first began among Roman soldiers. Do you think they had ringers and leaners?

HISTORY MYSTERY

What is the Great Wall of China, when was it built, and what's so amazing about it?

Answer: Begun in 215 B.C., the Great Wall of China is 1,450 miles long! The Chinese built it to keep out their enemies. It's the only thing built by people that is big enough to be seen from outer space. You can visit the Great Wall today if you go to China.

Alexander the Great

Philip II was ruler of the most powerful state in Greece. After he was murdered in 336 B.C., his 20-year-old son, Alexander, became ruler. By the time he was twenty-two, Alexander had led his armies into Persia and defeated King Darius.

From Persia, Alexander's forces moved through Asia Minor, Egypt, Afghanistan, and India. Everywhere they went they took the Greek culture and language with them.

Alexander the Great, as he was called, wanted to capture the whole world and rule it. His empire was the largest in the ancient world. It covered everything from Greece in the West to India in the East. He built great cities all through his empire. And he treated the people he conquered with respect. The most famous city he built was named for him. It was called Alexandria and was on the Nile River in Egypt.

In 323 B.C., when Alexander was only thirty-two years old, he became sick with a very high fever and died. He had hoped to unite all the different peoples in his land into one, but he died before he could make it happen.

When Alexander died, his great empire was divided among his generals who could not agree. The period of time from Alexander's death until about 30 B.C. is called the Hellenistic Age. It comes from the word "Hellene," which means Greek. Later, the kingdom of Greece was defeated by the Romans.

Maccabean Revolt; Persia Falls

330 B.C. ⟶ 143 B.C.

336 B.C.—Philip II is assassinated; Alexander the Great succeeds him as king of Macedonia.

333–327 B.C.—Alexander conquers Syria, Phoenicia; Egypt, Persia, and India; he died in 323 B.C.

300 B.C.—Greek mathematician Euclid is active.

264 B.C.—Carthage occupies Sicily, beginning the first Punic war with Rome.

239 B.C.—The appearance of Halley's comet is recorded for the first time.

200 B.C.—Iron horseshoes came into use.

200 B.C.—Parchment came into wide use.

Maccabean Revolt;
Persia Falls

Rome Rules Jews under
Augustus Caesar

Jesus is
Born

330–143 B.C.

135–7 B.C.

6–3 B.C.

264 B.C.—
Contests
between gladi-
ators are held
in Rome by
this time.

140 B.C.—Han Wu Ti
(martial emperor
rules the Han
dynasty in China.

100 B.C.—The Anasazi culture begins
to flourish in North America.
58 B.C.—The Gallic Wars
begin when Julius Caesar
invades Gaul.

12 B.C.—The Romans
attempt to conquer
Germany.

At Peace in Rome

135–7 B.C.

History & Politics

- 100 B.C. Rome. The famous Roman ruler, Julius Caesar, was born. About 1,600 years later, he was remembered in a play called *Julius Caesar*, written by Shakespeare.

- 73–71 B.C. Italy. A slave named Spartacus led the slaves in an attack against their masters.
- 48 B.C. Egypt. Julius Caesar's Roman army attacked Ptolemy XIII and defeated him. Caesar appointed his lover,

*J*ust as the Jews had thought would happen, in 63 B.C. the Roman army attacked Palestine and captured Jerusalem. They were led by one of their greatest generals, Pompey. For the next few years, the Romans fought among themselves, changed rulers often, and finally appointed a man named Herod as King of Judea (the new name for Palestine).

A Time of Peace

By that time Octavian had become ruler of the Roman Empire. He was called Augustus Caesar by the Roman Senate. His reign set up a 200-year period of peace and wealth in Rome. The Jews also had good government under the Romans. God was truly working to prepare the perfect time to send his Son Jesus into the world.

Herod

Other important things were happening during this time when the Bible was silent, too. King Herod helped the Jews rebuild the Temple in Jerusalem again, because it had almost been destroyed by cruel King Epiphanes. But Herod was also making sure no one else could take his kingship away from him. He even murdered his own wife and brother-in-law so they couldn't attack him.

Cleopatra VII, as ruler of Egypt.

- 44 B.C. Rome. Julius Caesar was killed on March 15. His nephew, Octavian, began his 58-year reign as leader in Roman politics.
- 40 B.C. Judea. Herod the Great was appointed King.
- 31 B.C. Egypt. On September 2, Augustus Caesar defeated Antony and Cleopatra in the famous battle of Actium.
- 30 B.C. Egypt. Antony and Cleopatra VII killed themselves at Alexandria.

Religious Groups

Also during this time the Jews had begun to divide into religious groups that believed different things about God and life after death. They no longer agreed on what God's words meant or how to follow him. The three main groups of religious Jews were called Pharisees, Sadducees, and Essenes.

Pharisees. The Pharisees were thought to be the most important of the three groups. They were the religious leaders of the Jews. They were very strict about following every detail of the law of God. But they also thought their religious traditions were as important as God's commands.

Literature & Theater

- 125 B.C. Egypt. A Jewish author in Alexandria wrote a fictional letter (The Letter of Aristeas) about the Hebrew Bible being written in the Greek language. He was trying to show that the Jews and Greeks could live together in peace.
- Cyrene. Jason wrote a five-book story of the Maccabees' war against King Epiphanes and the Seleucids. The story showed how God and the Jews who loved him won the war.
- Rome. Vitruvius published his work called *On Architecture*.
- Judea. A collection of poems was put together by the Pharisees and titled *Psalms of Solomon*.

- 100 B.C. China. Shadow puppets were developed.
- 59 B.C. Rome. Julius Caesar published the first public news bulletin. This was the first kind of newspaper ever published.
- 55 B.C. Rome. The first Roman playhouse was built. It was called Pompey's Theater.
- 47 B.C. Egypt. The great library at Alexandria burned. Much ancient writing was lost forever.
- 29 B.C. Rome. The poet Vergil began writing his *Aeneid*.
- 23 B.C. Rome. Horace, the great lyric poet, wrote his three books of 88 Odes. An ode is a poem that is meant to be sung.
- 20 B.C. Marcus Verrius Flaccus wrote the first dictionary of ordinary words.

Religion, Philosophy & Learning

- 124 B.C. China. A man named Han Wu Ti began a university for studying the teachings of Confucius. He also set up a written test for all Chinese people who wanted to work for the government. These people are called civil servants. The test was used for hundreds of years until A.D. 1905.
- 100 B.C. Rome. A system of education for both boys and girls was first developed.

Traditions are special ways people do things. These are passed down by word of mouth from parents to children to grandchildren. For instance, maybe some people always ate lamb chops on Monday. God didn't command them to do that, they had just always done it that way. It was a tradition. In truth, traditions are not as important as God's commands. So when traditions become rules, they are really false rules.

The Pharisees were known for certain things they believed. They believed that obeying every detail of the law of God made them more important to God. They also believed that people's spirits lived on after their physical bodies died. This was called life after death. Many Jews believed this; so the Pharisees had great support from the people. They were chosen most often to be government officers. They also served in the Sanhedrin—the most important group among the Jews.

Sadducees. The Sadducees did not believe that people had life after death. They also did not believe in following word-of-mouth traditions. They only accepted the written laws of God. And they tried to reason out everything about religion, as they had been taught to do by their Greek friends.

Essenes. This religious group is not mentioned in the Bible itself, but they were well known in Jewish society. The Essenes lived a simple life of sharing everything they had with each other. They were very strict about how their people acted, and most of them never married or had children. They lived together mostly in villages, but a few of them lived in the cities. They were also very strict about God's command to keep the Sabbath holy.

It's a
FACT!

God's Word teaches
that there really is
life after death.
The Sadducees did not
believe this,
and that's very
"sad, you see."
The Pharisees did
believe this,
and that's very
"fair, you see."

- 63 B.C. Judea. General Pompey captured the Temple of God in Jerusalem. Hundreds of Jews were taken to Rome as slaves.

- 20–18 B.C. Judea. King Herod had the Temple of God rebuilt in Jerusalem, using over ten thousand workers and priests.
- 8 B.C. Judea. Joseph and Mary (future parents of Jesus) probably became engaged to be married about this time.

- 8 B.C. Judea. Zechariah saw a vision of the angel Gabriel, who promised that Zechariah's wife, Elizabeth, would have a baby. They were to name the baby John . He became known as John the Baptist

Visual Arts

25 B.C.–A.D. 14. Rome. Augustus Caesar changed the buildings in the city of Rome from brick to marble. It became one of the most beautiful cities in the world.

Music

- 50 B.C. Rome. The musical instrument called the oboe was invented. This instrument is still used in orchestras today.
- 38 B.C. China. The Chinese musical octave was divided into sixty notes for the first time.

Science, Technology & Growth

- 130 B.C. Sidon. Antipater first listed the Seven Wonders of the World (see list on page 182).
- 127 B.C. Ptolemy began his book of amazing facts about astronomy called *Almagest*.
- 117 B.C. Egypt, India. Eudoxus of Cyzicus sailed from Egypt to India.
- 100 B.C. China, India. The first ships from China also reach India.
- 100 B.C. Syria. Glassblowing was invented. Syrian glassmakers found a less expensive way to make glass containers than by hand molding them. They put a blob of melted glass on the end of a long pipe and then blew through the other end. This formed a bubble that could be shaped and cut to make bottles. You can see still glassblowers today in such places as the famous Waterford Crystal factory in Ireland.
- 85 B.C. China. A seed planting machine was invented.

Other groups. Some other groups of religious Jews also began during this time, such as the Zealots, the Herodians, and the Samaritans. Each group had their own set of rules and beliefs. Each group thought it was the only one who was right with God. But each group was only a section of the nation of Israel.

When Jesus was born at the end of this period of time, he found all these different religious groups among the

Jews. They were divided, and they spent much time quarreling and fighting. They didn't agree about what God's word said or meant. And they didn't agree about who Jesus really was.

History Mystery

What was the first kind of gymnastics performed?
Answer: The first gymnastics were like circus acrobats. Between 200–100 B.C. the men and women of Minoan Crete developed the sport of bull leaping. In bull leaping the gymnast ran toward a charging bull, grabbed its horns, and when tossed into the air, performed midair stunts before landing on the bull's back. Then they dismounted with a flip. (Don't try this at home!)

- 85 B.C. Greece. The grain mill was invented. This meant that people no longer had to grind their grain by hand.
- 46 B.C. Rome. The Julian 365-day calendar and Leap Year were put into use.
- 40 B.C. China. The rotary winnowing machine was invented. A winnowing machine is used to separate good grain from the stalks and husks of the grain.

Daily Life

- 100 B.C. Rome. The first wedding cake was developed. But instead of the cake being served to the bride as it is today, it was thrown at the bride by all the guests at the wedding! It was the Romans' strange way of wishing the bride good luck in having lots of children.
- 100 B.C. South America. The cocoa plant was being cultivated. Chocolate is made from cocoa. Do you think Jesus might have eaten some chocolate or had hot chocolate on a cold night?
- 200–100 B.C. Egypt. Gymnastics were first begun.
- 100 B.C. Japan. Women dove to the ocean floor to get food. They had to hold their breath for as long as three minutes!
- 23 B.C. Japan. The first recorded wrestling match took place.

Apocryphal Writings

From about 200 B.C. to A.D. 100, writers often used a kind of writing called apocalyptic. This kind of writing used a lot of hidden meanings and symbols. It was like reading something written in a secret code. If you knew the secret code, then you could understand the message. But if you didn't know the code, the message seemed strange and didn't make any sense.

The Jews and early Christians, who lived during this time, shared many symbols that they understood very well. (See "Symbols of Christianity" on page 254) But their neighbors, such as the Romans, did not understand the secret symbols. So, Jewish and Christian writers sometimes used the symbols to send messages they wanted their own people to understand, but they didn't want the Romans to understand. These are the books of the Bible that are known as apocalyptic. Many of the books of the Apocrypha between the Old and New Testaments were also written this way.

Two of the most famous apocalyptic writings in the Bible are the Book of Daniel and the Book of Revelation. In these books we see many symbols, dreams, and visions. Some of the symbols were word pictures, and some were numbers. The people of that time probably understood the messages of these two books very well because they understood the symbols. Today, we find these books more difficult to understand because we don't always know what some of the symbols meant.

We'll try to discover the secret code of Revelation when we get to it near the end of this book. Meanwhile, see if you can solve this coded message:

!elpoep sih ♥ doG
!U ♥ doG dnA

Rome Rules Jews under Augustus Caesar

130 B.C.—The poet Antipater of Sidon lists the Seven Wonders of the World.

111 B.C.—The Han dynasty in China annexes Annam (northern Viet Nam).

100 B.C.—Bog burials are made in northern Europe around this time.

100 B.C.—Greek grammarian, Dionysius Thrax writes the Art of Grammar.

100 B.C.—The Anasazi culture begins to flourish in North America around this time.

82 B.C.—Roman general Sulla captures Rome and becomes dictator.

73 B.C.—The gladiator Spartacus leads an uprising of fugitive slaves in Italy.

60 B.C.—Pompey, Crassus and Julius Caesar form the first Roman Triumvirate.

58 B.C.—The Gallic Wars begin when Julius Caesar invades Gaul.

50 B.C.—Glassblowing is discovered around this time in Phoenicia.

46 B.C.—Julius Caesar is appointed dictator of Rome.

44 B.C.—Marcus Junius Brutus and Gaius Cassius Loninus assassinate Julius Caesar.

43 B.C.—Mark Antony, Marcus Aemilius Octavian (Augustus) and Lepidus form the Second Triumvirate in Rome.

29 B.C.—Roman poet Vergil begins the Aeneid.

27 B.C.—Roman emperor Augustus establishes the Praetorian guard.

18 B.C.—The Kingdom of Paekche is established in Korea.

THE NEW TESTAMENT

44 B.C.—Julius Caesar is assassinated by Marcus Junius Brutus, and Gaius Cassius Longinus.

29 B.C.—Roman poet Vergil begins the Æneid.

12 B.C.—The Romans attempt to conquer Germany.

6 B.C.—Judea comes under the direct control of Roman procurators.

1 B.C.—Roman poet Ovid writes the **Art of Love.**

6–3 B.C.

Matthew 2:2–10
Luke 1:26–28
Luke 2:1–20

Jesus Is Born!

History & Politics

- 6 B.C. Judea. The country of Judea and its people, the Jews, came under direct Roman control.

- 4 B.C. Judea. Herod the Great, who killed all the Jewish baby boys under age two trying to kill Jesus, died at age 69. This poem has been written about him:

> Herod then with fear was filled,
> "A prince," he said, "in Jewry!"
> All the little boys he killed
> In Bethlehem in his fury.

*T*he time had finally come. Everything that God had planned was in place. The eternal stage was set, and all the players were prepared to perform their assigned roles. God was ready to keep his promise to the Jews that he had made to Abraham over 2,000 years before. It was time for the Messiah to be born—the Son of God, the Savior of the world, the King of Kings and Lord of Lords, the Christ. And when the heavenly curtain went up, here's what happened.

An Angel's Message

*G*od sent an angel named Gabriel to visit a young woman who lived in the town of Nazareth in Galilee. Her name was Mary, and she was engaged to marry a man named Joseph. Joseph was from the family of King David of long ago.

The angel said to Mary, "Greetings! The Lord has blessed you and is with you."

But Mary didn't understand what the angel meant. So the angel said, "Don't be afraid, Mary, because God is pleased with you. Listen! You will have a baby boy, and you will name him Jesus. He will be great, and people will call him the Son of the Most High. He will rule over the people of God forever, because his kingdom will never end."

Mary said, "How will this happen? I'm not even married."

The angel said, "The Holy Spirit will come upon you, and the power of the Most High God will cover you. The baby will be holy. He will be called the Son of God."

BIBLE MYSTERY

Besides "Jesus," "Yeshua," and "Christ," what other name did Jesus have, and what did it mean?

Answer: "Immanuel" was his other name. It means "God with us." In other words, Jesus was really God himself who had come to earth as a man to live among the people he loved so they could get to know him better.

Literature & Theater

- 5 B.C. Asia Minor. Strabo wrote a survey of Greek geography.
- 2 B.C. Ovid wrote *Ars Amatoria*.

Religion, Philosophy & Learning

- 4 B.C. Judea. John the Baptist was probably born.
- Judea. The Jewish religion had split into groups (called "sects" or "sections"), such as Pharisees, Sadducees, Essenes, Zealots, Herodians, and others. See descriptions of these groups in "At Peace in Rome," page 210-215.

Visual Arts

India. Scenes from the life of The Buddha (see "The Buddha," page 168) were added to the Great Stupa stone sculpture at Sanchi's Gateway.

Judea. At the Temple musicians played cymbals and stringed musical instruments, such as the harp. Silver trumpets announced the beginning of events. Few ancient nations used music as much as the Jews did in their everyday lives.

Science, Technology & Growth

3 B.C. Galilee. A brilliant new star appeared in the eastern sky. Some scientists believe it was the one we call the Eastern Star.

Daily Life

1 B.C. Judea. Bringing gifts when visiting important people was a long-time custom. Wise men from far eastern countries brought such gifts to Jesus when they came to visit him.

Mary said, "I am the servant girl of the Lord. Let this happen to me as you say it will!" Then the angel went away.

The Birth of Jesus

Joseph and Mary had traveled to Bethlehem to list their names in a register as the emperor of Rome had commanded. While they were there, the time came for Jesus to be born. Since there were no rooms in the inn, Joseph and Mary stayed in a stable. And during the night, there in the straw, among the cat-

All the angels were praising God, saying, "Give glory to God in heaven, and on earth let there be peace to the people who please God."

Luke 2:13–14

tle, Jesus was born. It was the greatest moment in the history of all the world! And it happened in a barn.

Shepherds Worship Jesus

To announce his Son's birth, God sent a choir of angels to some shepherds who were taking care of their sheep in a field near Bethlehem. The shepherds hurried to the stable to worship the tiny king.

Wise Men Worship Jesus

God also put a bright new star in the eastern sky. And far, far away some wise men saw the star and knew that it was something very special. So they began

HISTORY MYSTERY

If you had a drachma, a shekel, and a denarii in your hand, what would you be holding?
Answer: Coins from the time that Jesus lived.

People and Their Names

Jewish people always thought a person's name was very important. They thought a name was more than something to call a person; it also told who that person was.

In the first century when Jesus was born, people often gave their children names of ancestors they loved or of great heroes. People often still do this today. One popular thing to do, especially for boys, was to add their fathers' names to the sons' names. For example, Paul Bar-John meant "Paul, son of John." Later, people began to shorten the way they said second names. So "Paul, son of John" became "Paul John's son." Before long, they shortened it even more to "Paul Johnson." Today we have lots of people whose last name is "Johnson." Many other names have come down to us that way, too, such as Peterson, Williamson, and Samson.

Jews also often had a second name, such as "Thomas, which is called Didymus." Thomas was this man's name in the Aramaic language, and Didymus was the same name in the Greek language. Both names had the same meaning, like Mary in English and Maria in Spanish. You will see some of these in your Bible.

Jesus' name in Aramaic was *Yeshua,* and that's what he was probably called by his family and friends. It was a popular name in those days. The name we call him,

traveling to where the star led them. The star was pointing the way to Jesus.

God had at last kept his wonderful promise. The Savior had come. But what would the world think of him? How would people treat him? Would they listen to him? And would they obey him? Only time would tell.

Did you know that...

it really took the wise men
about six months
to travel to where Jesus was?
They didn't visit him
in the stable.
The Bible says
they found him in a house.
(See Matthew 2:11)

Jesus Is Born	Joseph's, Mary's and Jesus' Flight to Egypt	Childhood of Jesus
6–3 B.C.	4 B.C.	2 B.C.

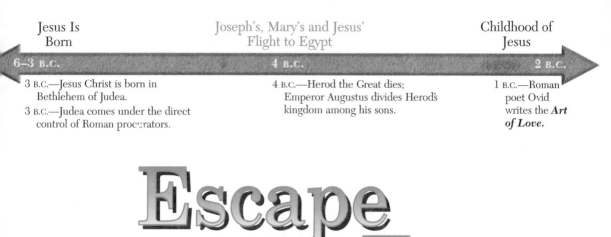

3 B.C.—Jesus Christ is born in Bethlehem of Judea.

3 B.C.—Judea comes under the direct control of Roman procurators.

4 B.C.—Herod the Great dies; Emperor Augustus divides Herod's kingdom among his sons.

1 B.C.—Roman poet Ovid writes the *Art of Love.*

Escape to Egypt

Matthew 2

3–1 B.C.

*A*fter Jesus was born, Joseph and Mary stayed with him in Bethlehem for several months. They moved from the stable to a house in Bethlehem. And the news about the birth of the Messiah, who was also called the King of the Jews, spread quickly.

Wise Men

The wise men had left their homeland about six months before this and finally arrived in Palestine where the star had led them. They probably thought, *Who would know more about a new king of the Jews (Jesus) than the old king of the Jews (Herod)?* So they went to see Herod at the palace in Jerusalem and asked him, "Where is the baby who

202 B.C. – A.D. 220. China. The Han Dynasty ruled.

225

was born to be the king of the Jews? We saw his star in the east. We came to worship him."

Herod Was Afraid

When Herod the Great heard there was a new king of the Jews, he was very worried. The Roman Senate had given Herod the title King of the Jews, because he ruled over Palestine where the Jews lived. He was afraid that this new king would replace him. That's not what God had planned, but Herod didn't know it.

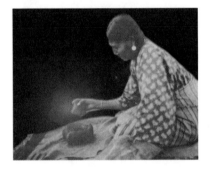
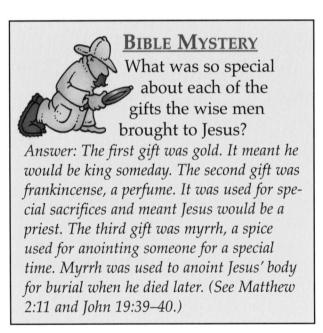

BIBLE MYSTERY
What was so special about each of the gifts the wise men brought to Jesus?
Answer: The first gift was gold. It meant he would be king someday. The second gift was frankincense, a perfume. It was used for special sacrifices and meant Jesus would be a priest. The third gift was myrrh, a spice used for anointing someone for a special time. Myrrh was used to anoint Jesus' body for burial when he died later. (See Matthew 2:11 and John 19:39–40.)

Herod asked the priests and teachers of the law where the Christ was to be born, according to Jewish teachings. They answered, "In the town of Bethlehem in Judea."

Then Herod had a secret meeting with the wise men. He asked them the exact time they had first seen the star in the eastern sky, and they told him it had been about six months before. So he said to the wise men, "Go to Bethlehem and look carefully for the child. When you find

Dᴉᴅ ʏᴏᴜ ᴋɴᴏᴡ ᴛʜᴀᴛ...

the Bible does not say
there were three wise men?
No one knows
how many wise men
came to visit Jesus.
We have always thought
there were three
because the Bible names
three gifts
that they brought.
(See Matthew 2:11.)

Science, Technology & Growth

- 206 B.C.–A.D. 220: China. The people of China believed that mirrors were magical and protected them from evil spirits. Mirrors were decorated with spirit beings and astronomy patterns.
- China. Salt mining was developed.

Daily Life

- 1 B.C. The people of Gaul began wearing Roman style clothes, such as togas. They also began shaving their beards.
- North America. Hunters in the southwest carried their hunting gear in animal-skin bags. These hunters belonged to the Anasazi people.
- Middle East. Groups of people traveled on camels across the Arabian deserts to bring sweet-smelling gums of balsam, frankincense, and myrrh. These were used to make perfumes.
- Rome. Kitchens had metal saucepans and strainers, wooden spoons, and pottery pastry molds.

What Is a Synagogue?

In Jerusalem was the beautiful Temple of the Lord, which Herod the Great had rebuilt for the Jews. All Jews tried to go there to worship God when they could, especially on certain holy days and for special feasts, such as the Passover.

In most smaller towns and villages there was also a synagogue by the time Jesus was born. The word *synagogue* means "place of meeting." The Jews didn't offer sacrifices at the synagogue, but it was the local place where they met to worship and to study the Law of Moses.

On the Sabbath day (this would be our Saturday), the Jewish people would meet to listen to someone read from the Law of Moses and explain what it meant. In the synagogue, the men sat on one side, and the women and children sat on the other side.

But the synagogue was more than a place of worship. It was the local school, the town meeting hall, and the meeting place of local government officers. The rulers of the synagogue were usually also the city rulers. They were to guard the people's actions and keep them right with God.

Today many churches use their buildings like synagogues. They have schools in them and have meetings and gatherings of all kinds. Our churches today are the centers of our daily lives, just like the synagogues in Nazareth where Jesus grew up.

him, come back and tell me. Then I can go worship him too." (Herod didn't really want to worship Jesus; he wanted to kill him!)

As the wise men left the king, the star appeared in the sky to lead them again. They followed it to Bethlehem, and it stopped over the house where Jesus was. After the wise men gave Jesus wonderful gifts of gold and perfume and worshiped him, they left.

Escape to Egypt

Then an angel of the Lord warned Joseph in a dream to take Mary and

The angel said, "Get up! Take the child and his mother and escape to Egypt."

Matthew 2:13

Jesus to Egypt. He said to stay in Egypt until the angel told them to return. So they got up in the night and left for Egypt.

Herod's Plot

When Herod saw that the wise men had tricked him, he was very angry. So he gave an order to kill all the baby boys in Bethlehem who were two years old or younger. But God had protected his Son Jesus. And he lived to become the Savior of the world.

BIBLE MYSTERY
What was another name for wise men at this time?
Answer: Magi.

Joseph's, Mary's and Jesus' Flight to Egypt	Childhood of Jesus	John the Baptist
4 B.C.	2 B.C.	A.D. 1–27
4 B.C.—Herod the Great dies; Emperor Augustus divides Herod's kingdom among his sons.	1 B.C.—Roman poet Ovid writes the **Art of Love.**	A.D. 4—Roman emperor Augustus adopts Tiberius and recognizes him as his successor.

A.D. 1–26

Matthew 2:19–23
Luke 2:39–52

Jesus Lost and Found

History & Politics

- The population of the world at this time was about 250 million people.

- A.D. 9. Rome. Titus Livius, called Livy, a historian from the city of Padua, finished his 142-book *History of Rome.* The work covered Rome's development from its foundation to the days of Augustus Caesar.

- A.D. 14. Rome. Tiberius became emperor.

*A*fter Herod the Great died in Judea, an angel of the Lord spoke to Joseph in a dream. The angel told Joseph to take Mary and Jesus back to their homeland because the people who were trying to kill Jesus had died. So Joseph and Mary took Jesus back to their own town of Nazareth in Galilee.

There Jesus began to grow up. He became stronger and wiser, and God blessed him. The Bible doesn't tell us much about Jesus as a boy. The next time Jesus appeared in the Bible, he was twelve years old. And he was in Jerusalem with his parents celebrating the Jewish Passover feast. At age twelve Jesus had to begin learning the Law of Moses and obeying it. But Jesus understood the Law much better than other boys his age. And that's why an interesting story is told about Jesus at age twelve.

Lost!

When Mary and Joseph started home to Nazareth from the Passover feast in Jerusalem, they thought Jesus was with some of their relatives who were traveling with them. But Jesus had stayed behind in Jerusalem, and Mary and Joseph didn't know it. After they had traveled a whole day, they began looking for Jesus among their friends and family. But no one had seen him. Jesus was lost!

Found

Joseph and Mary hurried back to Jerusalem to find Jesus. They looked and looked for him for three whole days. They were surely very worried by that time. Finally, they found him at the Temple. He was sitting with the religious

HISTORY MYSTERY

Could Jesus have seen puppet shows when he was a boy?

Answer: Yes! At this time the Greek people were already making puppet dolls with arms and legs that moved.

Literature & Theater

- A.D. 1. Rome. The poet, Ovid, wrote The Art of Love.
- A.D. 8. Rome. Ovid finished his greatest poem, *Metamorphoses*.
- A.D. 17. Asia Minor. Ovid died.

Religion, Philosophy & Learning

- A.D. 5. Cilicia. Saul of Tarsus, who later became Paul the apostle, was born.
- A.D. 6–15. Judea. Annas was appointed High Priest by the Roman governor. This is the first time that the High Priest of the Jews was appointed by the Romans.
- A.D. 19. Rome. The Jews are banished from Rome.
- A.D. 20. Judea. Saul of Tarsus came to Jerusalem to study with the great teacher, Gamaliel. See Acts 22:3.

Visual Arts

Rome. Bronze sculptures of the heads of important people were being made.

Science, Technology & Growth

- A.D. 1. Mexico. Picture writing (called "hieroglyphics") and the use of the long-count calendar were developing in the area of the Mayan people.

- A.D. 1. Columbia, Ecuador. Platinum smelting at very high temperatures was being done.
- A.D. 16. The first writing about diamonds.
- Rome. Homes of the upper middle class and wealthy people had a kind of central heating. Passageways beneath the floors (called "hypocausts") carried hot air that warmed the floors above.

Daily Life

- A.D. 6. Rome. Policemen and firemen first put into use by Augustus Caesar.
- A.D. 1–500. Rome, Egypt. Children were playing with rag dolls. Some of the dolls even had joints that would move.

teachers, listening to them teach and asking them questions. All the people who heard his questions and the answers he gave were amazed at how much he understood and how wise he was for his age.

When Joseph and Mary saw him, they were amazed too. Mary said, "Son, why did you do this to us? Your father and I were very worried about you. We have been looking for you everywhere."

Jesus asked, "Why did you have to look for me? You should have known that I would be here in the Temple where my Father's work is!" But they didn't really understand that he meant the work of God.

Growing Up

Then Jesus went with Joseph and Mary home to Nazareth. He always obeyed them and did as they asked him to do.

Jesus said, "Why did you have to look for me? You should have known that I must be where my Father's work is!"

Luke 2:49

Jesus continued to learn more and more and to grow stronger. People liked him, and he pleased God.

Jesus stayed in Nazareth with his parents, his brothers, and his sisters. He worked as a carpenter with Joseph until he was about thirty years old.

It's a FACT!

The age for a Jewish man
to begin being
a spiritual leader
was age thirty.
When Jesus reached
that age, he began
his work
as a minister.

BIBLE MYSTERY

Why was age twelve so important to a Jewish boy?

Answer: Age twelve was when Jewish boys were thought to be men.

The Marketplace

When you go shopping, where do you go? Do you go to a shopping mall or a huge grocery store? Well, when Jesus went shopping with his family for food, clothes, or other things, they went to the Jewish marketplace.

The marketplace was always a busy, noisy place. Located in a city street or open area, the marketplace was where all the sellers and buyers came together. Sellers displayed what they had to sell, and buyers walked along looking at the goods and buying what they needed. Sellers sold everything from wheat or barley to fish to bread and olives. Arab spice sellers offered special spices in small ready-to-carry bags. And weavers had rugs and warm blankets for sale. It might remind us today of an outdoor flea market or craft sale.

All kinds of sights, smells, and sounds filled the air in the marketplace. Sellers shouted out slogans to attract buyers, such as, "Fresh fish! Get your fresh fish!" or "Who will buy my hot bread today?" Sheep and goats bleated. Donkey's brayed. Sellers and buyers argued loudly about prices. And people laughed and talked to their neighbors and friends.

Every Friday, the day before the Sabbath, was an exciting day at the market for Jews. This was the day everyone came to buy the special things they would need to celebrate the Sabbath as God had commanded in the Law of Moses. Yes, going to the marketplace was exciting.

Childhood of Jesus

John the Baptist

Feeding of the 5,000

4–2 B.C.

A.D. 1

A.D. 27

1 B.C.—Roman poet Ovid writes the **Art of Love.**

A.D. 6—Judea becomes a province of Rome.

A.D. 8—Roman poet Ovid completes his greatest poetic achievement **Metamorphoses.**

A.D. 9—Chinese emperor Wang Mang founds the Xin dynasty.

A.D. 23—Emperor Wang Mang is killed.

A.D. 25—The Later Han dynasty is established.

Jesus Begins His Ministry

A.D. 27

Mark 1:9–11
Luke 3:1–18

History & Politics

A.D. **26–36.** Judea. Pontius Pilate was the Roman governor. He brought idols of the Roman emperor into Jerusalem, which made the Jews angry.

Literature & Theater

A.D. **14–68.** Italy. Racitus wrote his history, called *Annals,* which reported history from the time of Tiberias to the time of Nero.

*A*bout six months before Jesus was born, a baby named John was also born. John was probably Jesus' cousin. And he had a very special job to do for God. His job was to announce to the world that Jesus, the Savior, had come. As this story opened, John was preaching in Judea. He was telling people that they should change their hearts and lives and be baptized. That's why he was called John the Baptizer or, more often, John the Baptist.

Man from the Desert

*J*ohn was an exciting man to see and hear. He lived out in the desert most of the time. He wore rough clothes made of camel's hair, and he had a leather belt around his waist. Many people from Judea and Jerusalem went out to listen to John. They told about the sins they had done, and then they were baptized by John in the Jordan River.

This is what John preached to the people: "There is one coming later who is greater than I am. I'm not good enough even to kneel down and untie his sandals. I baptize you with water, but the one who is coming will baptize you with the Holy Spirit and with fire." He was talking about Jesus!

Some of the people asked John what they should do to be right with God. John said, "If you have two shirts, share with the person who does not have one. If you have food, share that too."

To the tax collectors, who often cheated people, John said, "Don't take more taxes from people than you have

Religion, Philosophy & Learning

A.D. 27. Judea. Jesus was baptized by John the Baptist and began his ministry.

Visual Arts

South America. Fancy goldwork, pottery, and textiles were being made in the Andes.

BIBLE MYSTERY

Who said that John the Baptist would be "a voice who calls out in the desert"?

Answer: The prophet Isaiah. And he said it hundreds of years before John the Baptist was even born!

Science, Technology & Growth

- A.D. 25–220. China. Ways of producing food greatly improved. All these farming tools were invented: seed drills, better plows pulled by two oxen, harrows, grain mills, winnowing machines, and winch-and-pulley systems for irrigation.

- Italy. Romans were using two types of water wheels to grind corn.

Daily Life

- A.D. 25–220. China. Padded saddles for horses were invented.

- Fishing was a popular occupation.

been ordered to take." And to the soldiers John said, "Don't force people to give you money. Be satisfied with the pay you get."

Jesus is Baptized

One day while John was preaching, Jesus came from his home in Nazareth to the Jordan River. He wanted John to baptize him. But John tried to stop Jesus. He said, "Why do you come to me to be baptized? I should be baptized by you!"

Jesus said, "Let it be this way for now, John. We should do all the things that are right." So John agreed to baptize Jesus.

God said, "This is my son, and I love him. I am very pleased with him."

Mark 1:11

After Jesus was baptized, he came up out of the river. At that very moment, heaven opened up, and Jesus saw God's Spirit, which looked like a dove, coming down on him. Then God's voice spoke from heaven and said, "This is my Son, and I love him. I am very pleased with him."

God will be pleased with us, too, if we change our hearts and lives and are baptized as he commanded.

DID YOU KNOW THAT...

John the Baptist
ate insects, called locusts,
and wild honey
as his food?
(See Mark 1:6.)

HISTORY MYSTERY

What kind of musical instrument was made from a sheep's horn?

Answer: The Shofar, which was blown like a trumpet to announce the beginning of special Jewish events.

Shepherds and Sheep

Many people in Jesus' time took care of sheep as a way of making a living. These people were called shepherds. The Jews had been shepherds for hundreds of years. Great men of Bible history, such as David and Moses, were shepherds. And there are still shepherds who care for their sheep in many countries today, such as New Zealand.

Kinds of shepherds. Some shepherds traveled around with their sheep, looking for good pastures and water, and they lived in tents. Other shepherds were poor people who lived in a village and kept their sheep nearby.

A shepherd's life. The life of a shepherd was hard. He spent most of the year outdoors in all kinds of weather, day and night. To keep warm in cold and wet weather, he wore a scarf around his head and a heavy mantle (cape) that was waterproof.

A shepherd's tools. The shepherd carried a staff with a large crook on one end, so he could reach over a cliff and pick up a lamb or sheep that had fallen. The shepherd also had a sling to protect himself and the sheep from wild animals. (See "Slings" on page 79) A shoulder bag (called a "scrib") was used to carry the shepherd's supplies. He usually had a leather bucket that folded up, and he had a light container for his own water. He often took a small musical instrument, such as a lap harp or flute, to keep him and the sheep company.

Jesus. Good shepherds loved their sheep so much that they would even die defending them if they had to. That's why Jesus is often called the Good Shepherd—he loves us so much that he was willing to die for us.

A.D. 9—German leader Arminius defeats three Roman legions in the Battle of Teutoburg Forest.

A.D. 14—Augustus dies; he is succeeded by Tiberius as emperor of Rome.

A.D. 23—Emperor Wang Mang of China is killed.

A.D. 25—The Later Han dynasty is established.

A.D. 28—John the Baptist is executed by Herod Antipas.

The Ministry of Jesus

A.D. 27–30

Matthew, Mark, Luke, and John

History & Politics

South America. The Andean civilization existed.

Literature & Theater

A.D. 28. Judea. Jesus preached the Sermon on the Mount, including the famous Beatitudes.

After Jesus was baptized, the Spirit of God sent him into the desert to be tempted by Satan. Satan tried hard to get Jesus to turn away from God, but Jesus avoided every temptation. He remained pure and holy.

Once his temptation was over, Jesus' preaching and teaching began. He traveled around the country to towns and villages to teach the people about God and about true worship. He did amazing miracles, and he told the people parables (stories with special meanings). The people loved Jesus, and many of them believed he was the Son of God and began following him.

Apostles

Early in his ministry, Jesus chose twelve other men to help him take the message about him to the people. These men were called apostles. They were ordinary men, such as fishermen and tax collectors. But Jesus knew that each one of them had been chosen by God to be a special messenger, just as the prophets had been long ago. They stayed with Jesus wherever he went. They heard him preach and saw his miracles. They were eyewitnesses!

Miracles

Jesus did many miracles during his ministry. He made people who were crippled able to walk, he made blind people able to see, he made deaf people able to hear. Jesus helped sick people get well, he made evil spirits come out of people, and he even raised dead people back to life! There was no doubt about it—Jesus was the Son of God! No one else could do such miracles as he did.

Religion, Philosophy & Learning

A.D. 28. Judea. John the Baptist was beheaded by Herod Antipas.

Visual Arts

Rome. Artists made jewelry, fine pots, and bronze jugs to be sold in other countries.

Science, Technology & Growth

A.D. 20. Greece. Strabo wrote his seventeen-book geography of all the world they knew about at that time.

Teachings

The people loved to hear Jesus teach, because he taught with power. His words were strong and sometimes hard to live by, but the people knew he was telling them the truth. So thousands and thousands of them believed that he was God's Son and followed him. One of his most famous teachings is called the Sermon on the Mount. You can read it in your Bible in Matthew 5–7.

Jesus also taught with parables. These are stories that have special meanings. They helped the people understand what Jesus was

Daily Life

- North America. Baby carriers were in use by the Anasazi people. They were made of light, bendable cradle boards padded with juniper bark, hides, or other soft material to cushion the baby's head. One of these baby carriers was found in Moqui Canyon, Utah, hundreds of years later.
- Rome. Pottery, bronze, and wooden kitchen tools were in use.

Mind Meld

Jesus went everywhere in Galilee. He taught in the synagogues and preached the Good News about the kingdom of heaven. And he healed all the people's diseases and sicknesses.

Matthew 4:23

preaching and teaching. You can read Jesus' parables in your Bible, too, in the books of Matthew, Mark, and Luke.

Trouble for Jesus

The leading priests and Pharisees became afraid of Jesus when so many thousands of people began following him. They thought he would take away their power over the Jews. So they began plotting a way to kill Jesus, even though he had done nothing wrong. They were planning something evil, but God was planning to use their evil for the good of the whole world. He was

It's a FACT!

Jesus used the words
of the Bible
to avoid Satan's
temptations.
And we can do
the same thing today.

Fishing and Fishermen

When Jesus chose his apostles, they left their jobs to go with him. Several of the apostles were fishermen because fishing was a popular way to earn a living in Jesus' time.

Eating fish. Because there were lots of fish in the Sea of Galilee, the Jordan River, and local ponds, the price of fish was low; so even the poorest people could buy fish for food. The Law of Moses said the Jews could eat clean fish, such as Tilapia and Sardine. But they could not eat unclean fish, such as catfish, eel, and lamprey.

Casting a net. Fish were most often caught with a casting net. The large net was thrown (cast) into shallow water. The net fell in a circle, and weights in the edges of the net pulled it down to the bottom of the water. As it went down, it trapped fish underneath. Then the fisherman pulled the net closed with a line attached to the center and brought it onto the shore.

Mending nets. Fishermen spent much time repairing their nets because they often got broken by the large fish they caught. They used long bronze needles threaded with cord. The cord was woven into the broken net and tied to give it strength.

Fishers of men. When Jesus asked Peter, Andrew, James, and John to follow him, he told them he was going to make them "fishers of men." In other words, they would bring people to God as they had brought fish to the shore.

planning to give up the One (Jesus) he loved so much, for the ones (us) he loved so much.

HISTORY MYSTERY

How did John the Baptist die?

Answer: His head was cut off! Because he preached against Herod Antipas for taking his brother's wife, Herod put John in jail. One night Herod's stepdaughter danced for him, and he liked it so much that he offered to give her anything she wanted. She asked for John's head on a platter. And Herod gave it to her.

BIBLE MYSTERY

What does Jesus' Greek name, Christ, mean?

Answer: It means "anointed one" or "appointed one." Jesus was appointed by God to be the Savior of the world.

Feeding of the 5,000	Jesus' Crucifixion and Ascension	Jesus' Resurection
A.D. 27	A.D. 29	A.D. 30

A.D. 23—Emperor Wang Mang of China is killed.
A.D. 25—The Later Han dynasty is established.

A.D. 28—John the Baptist is executed by Herod Antipas.

A.D. 30—Jesus Christ is crucified by order of Pontius Pilate, Roman governor of Judea.

The Saddest Day

A.D. 30

Matthew 26–27
John 18–19

A fter Jesus had preached for about three years, he went to Jerusalem to celebrate the Passover feast. When he came into town, thousands of people lined the streets to see him. They waved palm branches and shouted, "Hosanna!" (This word means "save now." They were asking Jesus to save them because they knew he was the Son of God.) So Jesus entered the Holy City as the King of Kings and Lord of Lords! Children sang. And the people bowed down and worshiped him. But this was to be Jesus' last journey.

The Last Week

During the next week in Jerusalem, Jesus often preached to the Pharisees and Sadducees about their evil ways. This made them angry, and they tried to think of a way to kill him. But they were afraid of what the people

History & Politics

A.D. 30. Rome. The city of Rome was the largest city in the western world with more than a million people living there. (See "The City of Rome" on page 188.)

243

Religion, Philosophy & Learning

A.D. 30. Jewish men wore talliths, which were prayer shawls. This was their way of showing that they were very religious.

Visual Arts

A.D. 1–50. The Celtic people made bronze artwork and furniture. Shields, mirrors, daggers, and dagger holders were decorated with swirling art patterns and flowers.

Science, Technology & Growth

South America. People in the Andes were using the llama to carry heavy loads, as the Jews used camels and donkeys. They also used the llama for wool and meat.

would do to them if they did. Then one of Jesus' own apostles, an evil man named Judas Iscariot, came to see the Jewish leaders. He offered to lie about Jesus so they could have him arrested and killed. They agreed to give him thirty pieces of silver for his lies.

Arrested

One day Jesus and the apostles had gone to a grove of olive trees called Gethsemane near Jerusalem. There Jesus went off by himself to pray. After he had prayed to God three different times, Judas Iscariot and some Roman

It's a FACT!

The reason Jesus healed people was so that everyone would know for sure that he was the Son of God. Only God can perform miracles. These miracles also teach us that we can come to Jesus and ask him when we need help.

soldiers came into the garden. And Jesus went out to meet them. Judas came up to Jesus and kissed him on the cheek. That's how the soldiers knew which man was Jesus. Then they arrested him.

On Trial

After that Jesus was put on trial several times. False witnesses, like Judas, told

BIBLE MYSTERY

What was the very first miracle that Jesus did?

Answer: He turned giant jars of water into wine at a wedding feast in Cana. See John 2:1–11.

What Are Miracles?

Are miracles magic? In Jesus' time people who worshiped false gods believed in magic. They tried to use spells and witchcraft to control their gods or other people. They thought magic could make other people love them. And they thought they could use magic to hurt or punish their enemies. In Deuteronomy 18:9–12, the Bible says that magic practices are wrong. And when people became Christians, they burned their books of magic, as it says in Acts 19:19.

Jesus' miracles. Jesus didn't use magic words or strange spells. Because he was God, he just spoke and what he said happened right away. The word *miracle* is a Latin word that means "wonderful thing." A miracle is a great event that can be done only by God's help. It's a special sign to show God's power.

Jesus did four different kinds of miracles. These four kinds of miracles showed that Jesus had power over these things.

1. *Nature.* He stopped a storm on the sea. He walked on water. And he made a little fish and bread feed thousands of people.

2. *Sickness.* He healed a crippled man. He made blind people see. And he made deaf people hear.

3. *Evil spirits.* Jesus commanded evil demons to leave people alone. And the demons had to obey him.

4. *Death.* Jesus brought people who had died back to life, such as his friend Lazarus and the daughter of a man named Jairus. Then he even came back to life himself!

There is nothing too hard for Jesus. And we should not be afraid to ask him for help when we need it.

lies about him. And finally, Pontius Pilate, the governor of Judea, handed him over to be killed, even though he knew Jesus had done nothing wrong.

Crucified

On Friday, the Roman soldiers took Jesus outside of Jerusalem to a hill called Golgotha. And there they cruelly nailed his hands and feet to a big wooden cross. After a few horrible hours of hanging on the cross, Jesus died. When he did, God made the sun go black, and the whole world was dark for three hours in the middle of the day. One sol-

dier said, "This man really was the Son of God!" And he was right.

Buried

Later, a man named Joseph, from the town of Arimathea, took Jesus' body down from the cross and buried it in his own new tomb. Everyone thought that was the end. Jesus was dead and buried. He hadn't saved them from the Romans as they had thought he would. And they began to wonder if he really was the Messiah after all.

But they were in for a great surprise!

Mind Meld

Jesus cried out in a loud voice, "Father, I give you my life." After Jesus said this, he died.

Luke 23:46

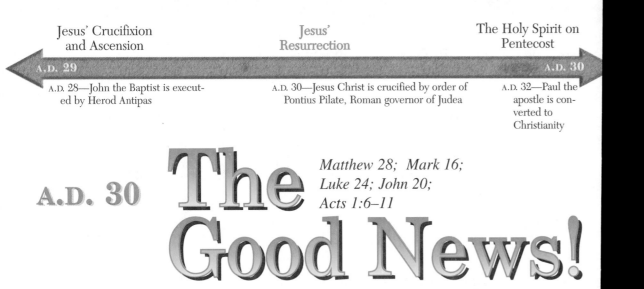

Jesus' Crucifixion and Ascension	Jesus' Resurrection	The Holy Spirit on Pentecost
A.D. 29		A.D. 30

A.D. 28—John the Baptist is executed by Herod Antipas

A.D. 30—Jesus Christ is crucified by order of Pontius Pilate, Roman governor of Judea

A.D. 32—Paul the apostle is converted to Christianity

The Good News!

A.D. 30

Matthew 28; Mark 16;
Luke 24; John 20;
Acts 1:6–11

*O*n Sunday morning, after Jesus was buried on Friday, a miracle happened! Just as the sun was coming up, one of Jesus' followers named Mary Magdalene and another woman named Mary went to Jesus' tomb.

The Angel

*S*uddenly there was a strong earthquake! And an angel from heaven came down and rolled the stone away from the door of Jesus' tomb. He was shining as bright as lightning. His clothes were as white as snow. The soldiers guarding the tomb were terrified of the angel.

He's Alive!

The angel said to the two Marys, "Don't be afraid. I know that you're looking for

History & Politics

4 B.C.– A.D. 39. Galilee. Herod Antipas governed Galilee. He was a good ruler for the Jews.

248

Jesus. He's not here anymore. He has come back to life! Go and tell his followers to meet him in Galilee."

The women left quickly to find the other followers. They were afraid, but they were so happy! Suddenly, Jesus met them and said, "Hello." The women came up to Jesus, bowed down, held his feet, and worshiped him. Then Jesus said, "Don't be afraid. Go and tell my brothers to go on to Galilee. They will see me there." So the women hurried away.

The Cover Up

The soldiers rushed into Jerusalem and told the leading priests everything that had happened. Then the priests and

HISTORY MYSTERY

What was a "tear bottle" in Jewish history? *Answer: "Tear bottles" were often put in a person's coffin with them. Legend says that people who cried for the dead person caught their tears in the little pottery bottles so they could be buried with their beloved one who was now dead. Psalm 56:8 says, "Gather my tears into your bottle."*

Religion, Philosophy & Learning

A.D. **30**. Judea. Christianity began when Jesus, the Christ, died, was buried, and came back to life. It has been followed by millions of people from then until now.

Visual Arts

Rome. Fine red pottery with a shiny surface was found in the homes of wealthy Romans.

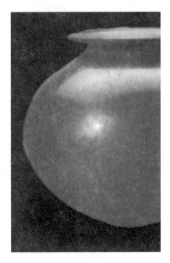

Daily Life

- Greece, Rome. Wine and expensive goods, such as bronze artworks, were traded to the Celtic people in Europe for cattle, skins, slaves, and salt.

- Judea. The Jewish people had many different kinds of baths. Some were for normal bathing, and others were for religious purposes.

BIBLE MYSTERY

Why did God let Jesus die on the cross? *Answer: Because God loved us so much. John 3:16 says, "God loved the world so much that he gave his only Son. God gave his Son so that whoever believes in him may not be lost, but have eternal life."*

older Jewish leaders made a plan to cover up the truth. They told people that Jesus' followers had come during the night and had stolen Jesus' body while the soldiers were asleep. And that story is still told to Jewish people even today.

Followers See Jesus

All the apostles, except Judas, met him in Galilee. Then he said to them, "All power in heaven and on earth has been given to me. So go and make followers of all people in the world. Baptize them in the name of the Father and the Son and the Holy Spirit. Teach them to obey everything I have told you. And I'll be with you all the way."

So go and make followers of all people in the world. Baptize them in the name of the Father and the Son and the Holy Spirit.

Matthew 28:19

Back to Heaven

A few weeks later, Jesus knew it was time for him to go back to heaven. So he said, "The Holy Spirit will come to you. Then you will receive power from God. You will tell everyone the Good News about me in Jerusalem, then in Judea, in Samaria, and in every other part of the world."

Then Jesus was taken up into heaven, and a cloud hid him from their sight. Then two men wearing white clothes said, "He will come back in the same way you saw him go." So the followers went back to Jerusalem to wait for him.

DID YOU KNOW THAT...

a Roman soldier was killed
if he went to sleep on the job?
That's why the story
about Jesus' body being stolen
while the soldiers
were asleep was impossible.

What Happened to the Law of Moses?

The Jews had finally completed the special job God had given them to do. Jesus had been born. So the Law of Moses, which God had given the Jews to keep them pure and holy until Jesus came, was no longer needed. The Old Testament of God was finished. When Jesus died on the cross, a New Testament of God was begun.

The Law fulfilled. The Bible says that the Law of Moses or the Old Testament was like a school teacher. It taught the Jews how to get ready for Jesus' coming. Now, the New Testament would be their guide for living as one of Jesus' followers.

In the Old Testament were many prophecies and promises about Jesus, the Messiah. When Jesus came, he was the answer to all those prophecies and promises. He finished the Law completely.

The wall came down. The Law of Moses had always been the reason that the Jews and their neighbors fought. It was like a wall between them. The Jews had to follow the Law of Moses, but everyone else still lived under God's law of good and evil. The New Testament of God is for all people everywhere; so there is no longer any reason for people to be divided. We can all be at peace under God's new agreement with us—the New Testament.

The Bible says this in Ephesians 2:14–16: "Christ made both Jews and non-Jews one people. They were separated as if there were a wall between them. But Christ broke down the wall of hate by giving his own body (on the cross). The Jewish law had many commands and rules. But Christ ended that law. Christ's purpose was to make the two groups of people become one new people in him. By doing this Christ would make peace."

Jesus' Resurrection	The Holy Spirit on Pentecost	Stephen Martyred/ Saul Converted

A.D. 30

A.D. 32–37

A.D. 30—Jesus Christ is crucified by order of Pontius Pilate, Roman governor of Judea.

A.D. 32—Paul the apostle is converted to Christianity.

A.D. 30

Acts 2—5

History & Politics

- A.D. 31. Rome. The Jews were allowed to return to Rome.
- A.D. 31. Italy. Nero, the Roman emperor, was put to death at Pontia.
- A.D. 33. Rome. Agrippina I starved herself to death.

Religion, Philosophy & Learning

A.D. 30. Jerusalem. Christianity began spreading quickly. See Acts 1:8.

Christ's Church Begins

*W*hen Jesus left the apostles and went back to heaven, he told them to wait in Jerusalem. The Holy Spirit was going to come and give them special power from God.

Pentecost

About fifty days after the Passover when Jesus had died, another feast happened. It was called Pentecost, or the Feast of Weeks. It was a time for the Jews to give offerings of thanks to God for their good crops. Because Pentecost was one of the Jews' three most important yearly feasts, thousands of Jews came to Jerusalem to enjoy the feast together.

252

The Holy Spirit

During the celebration the apostles were all together in one place. Suddenly, they heard a noise that sounded like a strong wind blowing from heaven. This noise filled the whole house where they were sitting. Then they saw what looked like tiny flames of fire over each person there. When that happened, the Holy Spirit came into each one of them. He made them able to speak foreign languages that they had never studied.

Some religious Jews were staying in Jerusalem. They were from every country in the world. When they heard the noise that sounded like wind, a huge crowd came together. And they were amazed because all of them heard their own languages being spoken.

They said, "Aren't all these men (the apostles) that we hear speaking from Galilee? But they are speaking every language in the world. How can they do that? What does this mean?"

BIBLE MYSTERY
Which friend did Jesus call "Rock"?
Answer: Peter. His name means rock.

Visual Arts

- A.D. 30. Narbonne. Triumphal Arch of Tiberius was finished.
- Rome. Architecture had decorated columns and arches. The Romans also used marble-covered floors and walls.

Science, Technology & Growth

- Rome. Ships had become the least costly way to trade goods with other countries. Roman trading ships were called "Corbitas."
- Africa. Lighting fires was probably done with fire drills. A piece of hard wood was rotated very fast in a piece of soft wood. This rubbing of the two woods together caused a spark that started a fire. Then fine, dry grass and leaves were added. Hunters in the Kalahari Desert still use this method of starting a fire today.

Daily Life

- Rome. Grain was shipped in for food from Egypt and North Africa.
- Rome. Wild animals were shipped in from Britain, Germany, and the Near East for the Roman circus.

Symbols of Christianity

In the days of Christ, Christians had symbols or signs that had special meanings to them. Sometimes these symbols were secrets that only the Christians understood. Here are some of the symbols and what they meant:

Fish. The outline of a fish was a symbol for Christ. Legend says that the fish was a secret symbol during the times that Christians were being persecuted. When two strangers met, one would draw half of the fish in the sand with his foot. If the other person drew the other half of the fish, then they knew both of them were Christians. Christians today still use this symbol. You may see it on the back of someone's car, which means that person is a Christian.

Palm leaf. The long leaf of a palm tree (called a "frond") was used as a symbol for Christ's victory over death. When Jesus entered Jerusalem before he died, the people waved palm fronds and shouted "Hosanna!"

Chi-rho. These two words stand for letters in the Greek alphabet. They are the first two letters in the name "Christ" in the Greek language.

Dove. The symbol of a dove stands for the Holy Spirit of God. Usually it is pictured flying downward, showing that the Holy Spirit came down from heaven to give power to Christians. This symbol is often still used by Christians today.

There are many other symbols with special meanings. These are just a few examples.

The Good News

Then Peter stood up, and the other apostles stood up with him. He spoke to the crowd and told them the Good News about Jesus. Perhaps the other apostles repeated what he said in the other languages so all the people could understand; we don't know for sure. Peter said, "God has made Jesus both Lord and Christ. He is the man you nailed to the cross!"

When the people heard this, they were very sad. They asked the apostles, "What shall we do?"

Then the apostles told them, "Change your hearts and lives and be baptized, each one of you, in the name of Jesus Christ for the forgiveness of your sins." About 3,000 people that day

DID YOU KNOW THAT...

there were people from about seventeen different countries in Jerusalem for Pentecost? So the Good News was preached in seventeen languages that day! (See Acts 2:5–12)

believed what the apostles told them and were baptized.

Beginning of the Church

After that the apostles did many miracles among the people. And everyone felt great respect for God. All the believers stayed together and shared everything they had. They ate together, laughed together, and loved each other. They praised God, and all the other people liked them.

Every day more and more people were being added to the group of believers, which was Christ's church. All the people who had heard the Good News in their own languages went home and told their own people about Jesus, too. So the church spread quickly through all the world... just as God had planned it all along.

"More and more people were being saved every day; the Lord was adding those people to the group of believers."

Acts 2:47

What Is the Church?

The Bible says that Christ is the head of the church and "the church is Christ's body" here on earth (see Ephesians 1:23). In other words, Christ is in charge of the church, just as your head is in charge of your body and tells it what to do. As parts of Christ's church, we are supposed to act like parts of a human body.

Now a body is a very interesting thing. As long as all the parts do what they're supposed to do, and what the brain (or head) tells them to do, the body works well. All parts have to work together to accomplish things. For instance, if the hands want to pick up a book on the other side of the room, but the legs won't walk to where the book is, nothing happens. They have to work together.

The same thing is true in the church. We are all important parts of Christ's body (the church). We are his eyes, ears, hands, and feet here on earth. In order for the church to do great things in the world, we all have to work together like a human body. If we don't, nothing gets done for Christ.

Together we are the church, the Body of Christ on earth. Our special job as his Body is to tell the world the Good News about him so they can be saved, too. And if we all work together in peace and love, we can do the job he wants us to do.

The Holy Spirit on Pentecost	Stephen Martyred/ Saul Converted	Gentiles Become Christians
A.D. 30	A.D. 32–37	A.D. 34–38

A.D. 30—Jesus Christ is crucified by order of Pontius Pilate, Roman governor of Judea.

A.D. 32—Paul the apostle is converted to Christianity.

A.D. 37—Tiberius is killed; he is succeeded by Caligula as emperor of Rome.

Stephen and Saul

A.D. 32–37

Acts 6—9

History & Politics

A.D. 37. Gaius became emperor of Rome. At age four he was nicknamed Caligula, which means "little boots." They gave him this name because he wore tiny military boots when he was a child.

The Good News about Jesus spread quickly through Jerusalem. So many people were becoming Christians that the Jewish leaders were afraid. But they couldn't attack the apostles without the people getting angry.

Deacons

To make certain that food was given fairly to all the Greek-speaking women whose husbands had died, the church chose seven men to take care of it. One of these special servants, called deacons, was named Stephen. The Bible says that Stephen was "a man with great faith and full of the Holy Spirit."

Stephen Is Killed

Stephen was able to do great miracles. But some Jews were against him. They came and argued with Stephen. But the Spirit helped him to speak with much wisdom. His words were so strong that the Jews couldn't argue with him. So they paid men to tell lies about Stephen. The men said, "We heard him say things against Moses and against God!"

The high priest said to Stephen, "Are these things true?" Stephen reminded the Jewish leaders of how much God had loved and cared for them since the days of Moses. Then he blamed them for killing Jesus, the Messiah.

When they heard this, they became very angry. They took Stephen

Religion, Philosophy & Learning

Judea. Stephen became the first Christian martyr.

Visual Arts

206 B.C. – A.D. 220. China. Tall towers and pavilions were popular. One tower was 374 feet tall. They were built for lookouts, and they often had shiny bronze roofs.

Mind Meld

"Soon Saul began to preach about Jesus in the synagogues, saying, 'Jesus is the Son of God!'"

Acts 9:20

Science, Technology & Growth

Rome, Sri Lanka. These two countries began trading goods when a Greek merchant named Hippalus was blown off course on his way to Arabia by monsoon winds.

Daily Life

Rome. Silk fabric and spices were shipped in from the Far East.

outside the city and threw stones at him until he died. The men who stoned Stephen left their coats with a young man named Saul, who agreed to killing Stephen.

Saul Meets Jesus

Later, Saul was scaring Christians in Jerusalem by telling them he would kill them, too. Then he decided to go to Damascus to arrest Christians there also. On the way, a bright light from heaven suddenly flashed around him. Saul fell to the ground. A voice said, "Saul, Saul! Why are you trying to hurt me?"

Saul said, "Who are you, Lord?"

The voice said, "I am Jesus, the One you're trying to hurt." Then Jesus told Saul to go into Damascus and wait for someone to tell him what to do. But when Saul stood up to go, he was blind!

Saul's men led him into Damascus, and he waited three days. Finally, a Christian named Ananias was sent by God to see Saul. Then God made Saul able to see again. And he got up and was baptized right away. He became a Christian.

God had a special job for Saul to do, and soon Saul began to preach about Jesus in the synagogues. He bravely said, "Jesus is the Son of God!" Later we will see that Saul became the greatest preacher of all time.

DID YOU KNOW THAT...

Stephen was the first Christian martyr? A martyr is a person who chooses to die rather than give up what he believes. Stephen died rather than quit believing in Jesus.

HISTORY MYSTERY

What famous French woman became a martyr for her country in the 1400s?
Answer: Joan of Arc.

Christian Martyrs: Then and Now

Since the time of Stephen, many Christians have died because they would not give up their belief in Jesus as the Son of God. These people are called martyrs. And they deserve our highest respect and thanks. Almost all of the apostles became martyrs for Jesus. Here's how they probably died:

Matthew was killed in a city in Ethiopia.

Mark was dragged through the streets of Alexandria in Egypt until he died.

Luke was hanged from an olive tree in Greece.

John, after being put into a pot of boiling oil at Rome and not being hurt by it, died a natural death at Ephesus in Asia.

Peter was crucified at Rome. According to tradition, he asked to be crucified upside down, because he did not think himself worthy to die in exactly the same way Jesus had died.

James the Great had his head cut off in Jerusalem.

James the Less was thrown from the roof of the Temple and beaten to death with a club.

Philip was hanged against a pillar at Hierapolis in Phrygia until he died.

Thomas was stuck with a spear at Corarandel in the East Indies.

Bartholomew was killed by having his skin ripped off while he was still alive.

Jude was shot to death with arrows.

Simeon was crucified in Persia.

Paul had his head cut off in Rome by the cruel tyrant, Nero.

Today Christians in many parts of the world are still being tortured and killed for believing in Jesus. Please pray for God to bless these brave people. They will have a very special place in heaven.

Stephen Martyred/ Saul Converted	Gentiles Become Christians	Missionary Journeys of Paul
A.D. 32–37	A.D. 34–38	A.D. 45–47

| A.D. 32—Paul the apostle is converted to Christianity. | A.D. 37—Tiberius is killed; he is succeeded by Caligula as emperor of Rome. | A.D. 41—Caligula is assassinated; Claudius becomes emperor of Rome.
A.D. 46—Thrace becomes a Roman province. |

Non-Jews Become Christians

A.D. 34–44

Acts 10

History & Politics

- A.D. 41. Rome. Claudius became emperor. His wife, Messalina, tried to defeat him and marry her lover Silius. Claudius was warned about her plans. He had them both killed. Then he married his niece, Agrippina.

- A.D. 41. Judea. Agrippa was made king by Claudius.

- A.D. 43. England. The city of London was founded.

So far the Bible has been mostly about the Jews. People who are not Jewish are all called Gentiles, or non-Jews. And now the Bible begins to tell us about them, too.

When God talked to Abraham hundreds of years before this, he had promised that all the nations of the world would be blessed through Abraham and his family, not just the Jews. God loves all people exactly the same—both Jews and non-Jews, as this story shows.

Cornelius Has a Dream

About three o'clock one afternoon a non-Jewish man named Cornelius had a dream from God. Cornelius was a Roman officer of over 100 men. He was a good man who gave many gifts to poor people, and he often prayed to God. God heard his prayers. So in the dream an angel of God told him to send for the apostle Peter, who was in the city of Joppa. Cornelius sent three of his men to Joppa right away.

Peter's Dream

About noon the next day, Peter went up on the housetop to pray, and God gave him a special dream, too. Peter dreamed about a big sheet coming down from heaven. It was full of all kinds of animals, reptiles, and birds. A voice said, "Get up, Peter. Kill and eat."

Under the Law of Moses, some of the creatures in the sheet were not supposed to be eaten by Jews. So Peter said, "No, Lord! I have never eaten food that is unholy or unclean."

But the voice said, "God has made these things clean. So don't call them unclean!" This happened three different

---

HISTORY MYSTERY

Whose mother was Agrippina, who married Claudius of Rome?
Answer: Nero, the cruel Roman emperor, was her son.

Literature & Theater

A.D. 43. Rome. The Roman poet, Martial, was born.

Religion, Philosophy & Learning

China. Weights and measures were set.

Visual Arts

Jordan. The desert temple, Petra, has some of the world's most amazing rock-cut architecture. It was cut out of sandstone cliffs. Petra was the capital city of the Nabataean kingdom. It's wealth came from trading goods with other countries.

Science, Technology & Growth

A.D. 37–68. Rome. Pepper was shipped in from India by the shipload. It was used to hide the taste of bad meat in Rome.

Daily Life

A.D. 40. Central America. Some of the Arawak people rowed a canoe to the West Indies for the first time.

times. Then the sheet went back into heaven. About that time, Cornelius' men came and asked for Peter. So Peter came down and went with them to the house of Cornelius in Caesarea.

Non-Jewish Christians

When Peter arrived at the house of Cornelius, many people were there. They wanted to hear what God was going to say to them. So Peter told them the Good News about Jesus. Then the Holy Spirit came down on all the non-Jewish people there, and they began to speak foreign languages. It was just like the day of Pentecost in Jerusalem.

Mind Meld

"The Jewish believers who came with Peter were amazed that the gift of the Holy Spirit had been given even to the non-Jewish people."

Acts 10:45

That's how Peter knew that God was now offering salvation to non-Jewish people. That day Cornelius and everyone there were baptized and became Christians. And God kept his promise to Abraham to bless all nations through his family (Jesus). He blessed us that day, too!

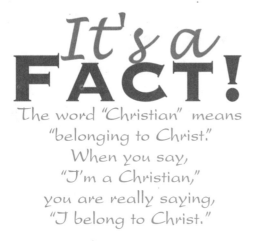

It's a FACT!

The word "Christian" means "belonging to Christ." When you say, "I'm a Christian," you are really saying, "I belong to Christ."

BIBLE MYSTERY

Who was the first non-Jewish Christian in Europe?
Answer: Lydia. The apostle Paul met her near the city of Philippi. See Acts 16:11–15.

Foods of the First Century

The Jews ate two regular meals each day. One was at noon, and the other was in the evening. Food was simple, but there was plenty for most people.

Types of food. The most common foods were fruits, vegetables, fish, dairy products (milk and cheeses), honey, eggs, nuts, and bread. Meat was usually eaten only on holy days (where we get our word "holidays").

Bread. Many kinds of grain grew in Palestine (Judea) where the Jews lived. So bread, which is made of grain, was the most common food of all. One kind of bread was a small, round loaf. Another kind was a thin, flat bread they simply called "cakes." The loaves were placed into a heated clay oven directly on the hot coals. The thin cakes were cooked on the outside of the oven.

Drinks. Milk was popular in Palestine because they could get it from their goats. They also drank wine, which was made from the grapes in their vineyards. And they had plenty of water from the streams and rivers.

Style of eating. Today we sit in chairs around tables to eat. But in Jesus' time, especially in wealthy homes, people lay on mats around a low table. They leaned on their left arm and ate with their right hand. Their heads were next to the table, and their feet were away from the table. Mats were usually placed on three sides of the table. The fourth side of the table was left open so the servants could wait on the people eating.

Gentiles Become Christians	Missionary Journeys of Paul	Letters to Churches
A.D. 34–38	A.D. 45–60	A.D. 61–64

A.D. 37—Tiberius is killed. He is succeeded by Caligula as emperor of Rome.

A.D. 43—The Romans invade Britain.
A.D. 50—The expansion of the kingdom of Aksum begins in present-day Ethiopia.

A.D. 64—Rome is devastated by fire; the Christians are blamed and persecuted.

On the Road with the Good News

A.D. 45–60

Acts 13–28

History & Politics

- A.D. 50. Germany. The city of Cologne was founded.

- A.D. 54. Rome. Nero became emperor when his mother, Agrippina II, poisoned Nero's father, Claudius.

- A.D. 47–120. Greece. The famous historian, Plutarch, lived and recorded history.

Literature & Theater

- These books of the Bible were probably written during this time: Matthew, Mark, John, Romans, 1 and 2 Corinthians, Galatians,

So that more people could be told the Good News about Jesus, the apostle Paul (Saul's new name) began to travel. He made three important journeys to many different cities and countries. There he preached and taught the people about the freedom Christians have as followers of Christ. He taught both Jews and non-Jews about the grace of God.

The Old Law

While Paul was traveling, some trouble started between the Jewish and non-Jewish Christians. The Jewish Christians believed that the non-Jewish Christians should obey the Law of Moses, as well as follow Christ. After following the Law of Moses for hundreds of years, it was very hard for the Jews to think that it was no longer needed.

Jerusalem Council

To settle the problem a meeting was held in Jerusalem. This meeting is known as the Jerusalem Council. The apostles and older Jewish leaders met to talk about the problem. After much talk, it was decided that the Jews should not make it hard for non-Jews to follow Christ. In other words, they agreed that the Law of Moses was not required for non-Jewish Christians.

Galatians

Shortly after the meeting in Jerusalem, Paul probably wrote the Book of Galatians. It was a letter from Paul to the Christians in the city of Galatia. In his letter he explained that Christians were not required to follow the Law of

BIBLE MYSTERY
What does the name Barnabas mean?
Answer: It means "son of encouragement." Paul's friend, Barnabas, was always trying to help other people.

Ephesians, Colossians, 1 and 2 Thessalonians, Philemon, James, and 1 Peter.

- A.D. 58–138. Rome. The famous poet, Juvenal, lived and wrote.

Religion, Philosophy & Learning

The apostle Paul made three historic missionary journeys to preach the Good News of Jesus.

Visual Arts

- South America. The Moche people were famous for their pottery.

- Germany. Glassmakers in Cologne became famous for their work.

Music

- A.D. 58–75. China. Three orchestras began to play in the courts. One orchestra played for religious events. One played for the archery in the palace. And one played for banquets and the emperor's women. A large military band was also in use.

- A.D. 60. Rome. The emperor Nero began having what he called "holy festivals." Music was most important at these festivals.

Science, Technology & Growth

- A.D. 50. Greece. A simple steam machine was invented by the Greek inventor, Hero. To Hero his machine was more of a toy than a real source of power.

- South America. Skilled Andean engineers built a network of roads over hills and mountains.

Moses anymore. He defended their freedom from the Law. He said that Christians had a new kind of agreement with God. And God had given them his wonderful grace.

Travels Continue

Paul traveled about for several years, preaching and teaching. During his travels Paul also wrote letters to many of the churches he had started. (We will talk about these letters in the next lesson.) Because Paul was popular among the people, the older Jewish leaders

The Holy Spirit said, "Give Barnabas and Saul to me to do a special work. I have chosen them for it" So they… laid their hands on Barnabas and Saul and sent them out.

Acts 13:2–3

were jealous. So they began making trouble for Paul. Finally, he was arrested and put into jail.

DID YOU KNOW THAT...

Paul wrote more
of the books
of the New Testament
than any other writer?

HISTORY MYSTERY

If you were using a cubit or a span, what would you be doing in Jesus' time?

Answer: You would be measuring something. A cubit was about eighteen inches— the distance from the end of a man's longest finger to his elbow. And a span was the width of a man's hand with his fingers spread apart. Other measurements were the palm and finger.

Daily Life

- A.D. 50. Rome. The Romans learn the use of soap for the first time from the Gauls. (Phew! What a relief!)

- Rome. Wine, olive oil, and fish paste were carried in pottery jars called amphorae, which could be packed tightly in the hold of a ship.

What Happened to Music?

During the first century A.D., very little is known about music. Does that mean that there was no music during the days of Jesus? Not at all. It just means that no one wrote much about what was happening in the area of music.

The early Christians sang psalms and hymns. We still sing some of the same hymns that Christians in the first century sang. Two of those songs are "*Adeste Fideles*," which we call "O Come, All Ye Faithful," and "*Gloria in Excelsis*." You may sing these at school or at church. The apostles may have sung them, too.

Jesus and apostles sang. We know that Jesus and the apostles sang hymns. After they shared the Lord's Supper, the Bible says in Matthew 26:30, "They sang a hymn. Then they went out to the Mount of Olives."

Paul and Silas sang. We also know that the apostle Paul sang songs to God, even when he was in jail. Acts 16:25 says that, "About midnight Paul and Silas were praying and singing songs to God."

The church sang. And we know that the early church sang different kinds of songs to help each other. In Ephesians 5:19 Paul tells the Christians at Ephesus to "Speak to each other with psalms, hymns, and spiritual songs. Sing and make music in your hearts to the Lord."

Music is one of the most powerful ways to teach the Good News to other people. It is a very special gift from God that we should use to praise and thank him.

Paul's Trials

Paul was asked to defend himself several times in front of different rulers and courts. Each time he told the truth about himself and about Jesus. In the end, Paul asked to be sent to Rome to tell his story to the Roman emperor, Caesar. As a citizen of Rome, Paul had that right.

While sailing to Rome, Paul's ship was torn apart by a storm that lasted two weeks. The shipwreck took place near the island of Malta. All the passengers got to shore safely because God saved them. They stayed on the island for three months, and Paul helped the people there. Then they sailed on to Rome on a different ship.

During Paul's journeys, thousands of people became Christians, and the church grew stronger everywhere he went.

Missionary Journeys of Paul	Letters to Churches	Paul & Peter Persecuted and Martyred
A.D. 45–60	A.D. 61–64	A.D. 64–95
A.D. 50—Cologne is founded in present-day Germany.	A.D. 62—James, the brother of Jesus, is stoned to death.	A.D. 64—The Kushans sack the city of Taxila in present-day Pakistan. A.D. 75— Josephus begins his history of the Jewish War.

Letters To the Churches

A.D. 61–64

Romans–Philemon

When Paul arrived in Rome, he was not taken to see Caesar. He was allowed to rent a small house and live by himself. He wasn't put into prison, but he was guarded by a Roman soldier. Paul lived there for two years. During that time Paul was also allowed to have visitors and to preach and teach about Jesus. No one tried to stop him. So he invited many people to come to his house, and he spoke bravely about Jesus.

Writing Letters

During Paul's travels and his house arrest in Rome, he also wrote letters to the churches he had started during his travels. The four letters that he wrote while in Rome are sometimes

History & Politics

A.D. 64. Rome. A huge fire rages through the city of Rome for nine days. It began on July 18. The Roman emperor, Nero, blamed the Christians for the fire. Then he began very cruel treatment of them. This was the first time that Christians were labeled as bad by the Roman government.

269

Literature & Theater

These books of the Bible were probably written: Luke, Acts, Philippians, 1 Timothy, and Titus.

Religion, Philosophy & Learning

- A.D. 62. James, the brother of Jesus, was stoned to death.
- A.D. 64. Rome. The first bad treatment (persecution) of Christians.

Visual Arts

Rome. Wealthy people often had Mosaic patterns to decorate their living-room floors.

called the Prison Epistles, because he wrote them while he was under house arrest.

Special Letters

Some of Paul's letters were written to special people, such as the Book of Philemon. Philemon had a slave named Onesimus, who had run away. Onesimus came to Rome, and there he met Paul. Paul taught Onesimus about Jesus, and Onesimus became a Christian. Then Paul sent him back to Philemon with the letter we call the Book of Philemon. In the letter Paul asked Philemon, a Christian, to take Onesimus back, not as a slave, but as a brother in Christ. The letter from Paul to Philemon teaches us today how to treat each other.

DID YOU KNOW THAT...

the word epistle means "to send to"? The New Testament has twenty-one epistles, which is really just a big word for letters. You can write an epistle, too!

General Letters

Some of Paul's other letters were written to all the churches. In those days, a letter was read by one church. Then it was sent on to another church. Then to another, until all the churches had read it. Most people believe that the Book of Ephesians was a letter for all the churches. In that letter Paul showed how

Mind Meld

"From Paul, a servant of Christ Jesus. God called me to be an apostle and chose me to tell the Good News."

Romans 1:1

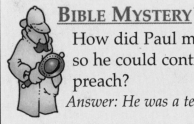

BIBLE MYSTERY

How did Paul make a living so he could continue to preach?

Answer: He was a tentmaker.

Daily Life

A.D. 61. Rome. Human sacrifices were no longer legal as part of evil Halloween celebrations.

Slaves and Slavery

In the first century when Paul lived, slaves like Philemon were common. In wealthy homes in Palestine, slaves worked mostly as servants in the big houses. They would be like maids and cooks today.

Jews could become slaves in three different ways. Sometimes Jews would sell themselves into slavery to pay off a debt they owed or because they were so poor. Or, if Jews were caught stealing, they might have to become slaves to pay back what they had stolen.

The third way was for a Jewish father to sell his young daughter into slavery as a servant in the house of another Jew. His hope was that she would marry into the family she worked for at the right age. But on her twelfth birthday, if she hadn't married, she was returned to her father's home. No Jew could own an adult Jewish woman.

The Romans were often very cruel to their slaves. Even Roman women were mean to the servant girls who helped them. Slaves who did something wrong were often beaten with scourges—leather whips.

Jewish slave owners often treated foreign slaves badly. But Jewish slaves were often treated as part of the family.

In many countries today people still have slaves. Some are treated fairly, but others are not. The Bible says that we should all think of ourselves as slaves to Jesus, and we should let him be the master of our lives. Because he loves us so much, we know we will be treated with love and gentleness.

Jesus was the answer to God's promises and plans from the beginning of time. The letter also talked about a Christian's friendship with God.

Messages of the Letters

Each letter that Paul wrote had a special purpose. Sometimes he wrote to help churches work out problems they were having, such as Philippians and Corinthians. Other times he wrote to teach someone how to do something. His letters to Timothy and Titus, who were preachers, were to help them know how to set up churches. Other letters were written to teach Christians how to live the right way.

Even though these letters were written hundreds of years ago, they are still our very best guide in how to live for Christ today.

HISTORY MYSTERY

Who really burned down the city of Rome?
Answer: Legend says that Nero set the fire himself and then played his violin while he watched it burn. But no one really knows for sure who set the fire.

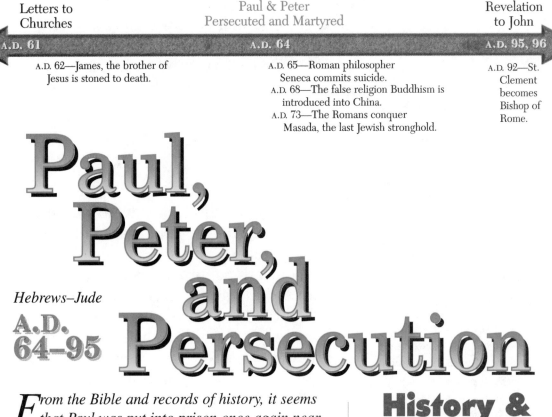

A.D. 62—James, the brother of Jesus is stoned to death.

A.D. 65—Roman philosopher Seneca commits suicide.
A.D. 68—The false religion Buddhism is introduced into China.
A.D. 73—The Romans conquer Masada, the last Jewish stronghold.

A.D. 92—St. Clement becomes Bishop of Rome.

Paul, Peter, and Persecution

Hebrews–Jude
A.D. 64–95

*F*rom the Bible and records of history, it seems that Paul was put into prison once again near the end of his life. Then he became a martyr for Christ (see "Christian Martyrs: Then and Now" on page 259). No one knows for sure how Paul died or where, but it's certain that he gave up his life rather than give up his belief in the Lord.

Non-Paul Letters

Not all the letters in the New Testament were written by Paul. Some were written by Peter, James, Jude, John, and others. From Peter's two letters (1 and 2 Peter), we can tell

History & Politics

- A.D. **66.** Judea. The Jews began to revolt against Roman rule.
- A.D. **68.** Rome. Emperor Nero killed himself.
- A.D. **69.** Rome. Vespasian became emperor.
- A.D. **70.** Judea. Jerusalem was destroyed by the Roman army.
- A.D. **79.** Italy. On August 24 Mt. Vesuvius, a volcano, erupted. It buried the

273

two Roman cities of Pompeii and Herculaneum. People ran away in panic. Pompeii was buried under twelve feet of volcanic ash. Herculaneum was drowned in a torrent of volcanic mud.

Literature & Theater

- These Bible books were probably written during this time: 2 Timothy, Hebrews, 2 Peter, 1 John, 2 John, 3 John, Jude, and Revelation.
- A.D. 43–96. Rome. Suetonius wrote *The Lives of the Caesars*. He gives biographies of the Roman emperors from Augustus to Domitian. Suetonius was secretary to Emperor Hadrian; so his writings have special value.
- A.D. 75. The famous historian, Josephus, began his *History of the Jewish Wars*.
- A.D. 77. Pliny the Elder wrote his *Historia Naturalis*.

that Peter and Paul probably saw each other again in Rome. Peter also knew about Paul's letters and what they said. And, like Paul, Peter died as a Christian martyr.

Persecution

About this time Christians began to be treated very badly. Some were whipped, some were stoned, some were killed by wild animals. Some were made to fight to the death against prisoners and slaves. Others were tortured by being left in the hot sun to burn to death. Some were drowned in boiling oil. Still others were thrown into prison and left to die. It was a very hard time for Christians. Some of the New Testament letters were written to give courage to the Christians who were being hurt.

HISTORY MYSTERY

What famous painter later used the fresco style of painting, and what famous painting did he do?
Answer: Michelangelo used this method to paint the famous Sistine Chapel in Rome.

It's a FACT!

The Christians dug
long tunnels and rooms
in the soft rock
under the city of Rome.
They used them to bury
their dead and to hide.
They also met
in these rooms to worship.
These underground passages
are called catacombs.
There are about 600 miles
of catacombs
under Rome!

Hebrews

The Book of Hebrews was a letter of courage for hurting Christians. Some of the Jews who were being persecuted for becoming Christians were turning back to the Law of Moses.

Hebrews showed them how much better Christ was than the old law.

Religion, Philosophy & Learning

- A.D. 67. Rome. The two great apostles, Peter and Paul, were both martyred.
- A.D. 68. China. The religion of the false god Buddha was brought to the Chinese people.

- A.D. 70. Rome. The Jewish Zealots escaped to the fortress at Masada.
- A.D. 73. Masada. The Roman Tenth Legion captured Masada, but the Zealots had all killed themselves rather than be captured.

Visual Arts

- A.D. 80. Rome. The Flavian Colosseum was built in Rome. It took up six acres of land and had seats for 50,000 people, which was amazing in those days.
- Rome. Wealthy people had bright-colored walls in their houses.

The walls were painted with fake windows and columns to make the rooms feel bigger. Much of the painting was done while the wall plaster was still wet. That way the color soaked into the wall. This is called fresco painting.

- A.D. 81. Rome. The Arch of Titus was built.
- Rome. Wealthy people had fine glassware on their tables. One famous glassmaker was named Ennion.

Music

A.D. 70. Judea. Instrumental music disappeared. Music may have been sung a cappella, or without instruments, to keep their worship meetings from being heard by the Romans. Chants were still used by the Jews, too. These may have later been the basis of the famous Gregorian chants.

Science, Technology & Growth

- Italy. Balsam, which is the sap of a certain kind of bush, had antiseptic qualities and a nice smell. It was used to clean wounds.

- A.D. 71. Rome. Flush toilets were invented.
- A.D. 79. Rome. The compass for drawing circles was developed.

Who wrote the Book of Hebrews? No one knows for sure. Some people think it was Paul. Others think it might have been Luke or Barnabas or Apollos. But it's certain that the writer knew the pain and hurt the Christians were hav-

BIBLE MYSTERY
The apostle Paul said that he had a "thorn in his flesh." What was it?
Answer: No one knows for sure. Some people think Paul could not see very well. Others think he was short, bald, and ugly. Still others think he was crippled. Whatever it was, Paul was a great servant of God in spite of it.

ing to go through. So he reminded the Jewish Christians of all the great heroes of faith who had gone before them. He talked about Noah, Abraham, and Enoch. And he told them to stay faithful to God, no matter what happened.

False Teachers

The church was also having some problems with false teaching. People, who believed a teaching called the Gnostic philosophy, were telling false things to Christians in the church. So, some of the letters of the New Testament, such as 1 John, were written to help

- A.D. 80. China. Magnets were discovered.
- A.D. 90. China. The art of making paper was first developed. The paper was made from the soft part of wood called "pulp" and cloth rags.

Daily Life

- A.D. 79–88. Italy. A deadly disease spread through the country. In Rome over 10,000 people died in one day!

We have many people of faith around us. Their lives tell us what faith means. So let us run the race that is before us and never give up… Let us look only to Jesus… he makes our faith perfect.

Hebrews 12:1–2

Masada:
The Jews'
Last Stand

Masada is a Hebrew word that means "fortress." In Bible times, Masada was a fortress built on top of a very high mountain. It was about thirty miles southeast of Jerusalem, and it looked down on the Dead Sea. Herod the Great built a huge palace, storehouses, barracks for soldiers, water cisterns, and walls there. Because it was so far away from anything else, and because of its great, high cliffs, Masada was the strongest fortress ever built.

In A.D. 70 the Tenth Legion of the Roman army destroyed the city of Jerusalem and the Temple of God. One group of the Jews who fought against the Romans was called the Zealots. When Rome attacked Jerusalem, about 1,000 Zealot men, women, and children escaped to Masada.

The Roman army surrounded the Jews on the mountain of Masada, but they could not defeat them. The Zealots' leader was Eleazar ben Jair. He helped the Zealots stand up against the Romans for over two years.

When the Roman army finally found a way to attack Masada in A.D. 73, all the Zealots killed themselves rather than be captured and tortured by the Romans. Each man killed his own family; then the men all killed each other. The last man, Eleazar ben Jair, killed himself. This was the Jews' last stand against the mighty Roman army.

Masada is in ruins today. It was uncovered by an archaeologist from Israel named Yigael Yadin from 1963–65. Today Masada is both a popular tourist site and a national shrine in Israel.

Christians avoid those false teachings. These were general letters that were passed around among the churches.

All these letters helped the early Christians to remember how very much God loved them. From the time of Adam and Eve until the time of Peter and Paul, God had never stopped loving and caring for his people. And he had not forgotten his promise to save them.

Paul & Peter Persecuted and Martyred	Revelation to John	From Then till Now
A.D. 61–64	A.D. 95, 96	A.D. 96–2,000

A.D. 66—A Jewish revolt against Rome begins in Judea.
A.D. 68—Roman emperor Nero commits suicide.
A.D. 77—Pliny the Elder writes his *Historia Naturalis.*

A.D. 79—Mt. Vesuvius erupts, burying the Roman city of Pompeii.
A.D. 80—The building of the Colosseum is completed in Rome.

A.D. 1517—Theologian Martin Luther nailed his 95 theses to the church door at Wittenburg, Germany.

The Final Victory!

A.D. 95–96

The Book of Revelation

*W*ith Peter and Paul both gone, leadership of the early Christians fell to one man—the old apostle John. But the Roman emperor, Domitian, put John in prison on the Isle of Patmos in A.D. 95. He thought that by taking John away the other Christians would soon give up their faith in Christ, and the church would die. John lived the rest of his life on Patmos.

One Sunday John received a strange-but-wonderful dream from Jesus. An angel told John to write down everything he saw and to send it to seven churches in Asia. What John saw and wrote is what we call the Book of Revelation.

A Coded Message

*T*he Revelation of John is a secret message, written in apocryphal (coded) language (see "Apocryphal Writings" on page 216). It was written

History & Politics

A.D. 85. Rome. Domitian became ruler of the Roman Empire.

Literature & Theater

• China. Liquid ink was made by rubbing solid ink onto an ink-stone with water. Then a brush was used to put the liquid ink on paper.

•A.D. 96. Patmos. The Book of Revelation was probably written by Jesus Christ through John the apostle.

Religion, Philosophy & Learning

- A.D. 95. Rome. Domitian killed Flavius Clemens, a Roman consul. He accused Clemens of not believing in God. In truth, Clemens may have been a Christian that Domitian wanted to get rid of.
- A.D. 97. Ephesus. Paul's traveling friend and a preacher, Timothy, became a martyr.

HISTORY MYSTERY

Where is the lost city of Petra?

Answer: It's in the country of Jordan. It was rediscovered by a Swiss explorer named John Burckhardt. Petra was the home of the Nabatean people. Its buildings are carved out of the side of a rock mountain. That's why it's called Petra, which means "rock." This is the same name Jesus called Peter.

this way so that most Jewish Christians could understand it, but the Romans could not understand it. Then the Jewish Christians could tell the non-Jewish Christians what it meant.

At this time Christians were being attacked and hurt almost everywhere. They could not understand what had happened. Jesus had come and gone, but he had not rescued them from the Romans. Had Satan won the battle? Was the church going to be destroyed by evil? If not, when would God take charge? When would they be rescued? The Revelation was given to John to help answer these questions.

The Meaning

In John's amazing dream he saw God's plan from the beginning of time unfold. It began with God as the great Creator of the world—awesome and wonderful! Then he saw how people had sinned against God and were forced out of the Garden of Eden and away from God's presence. But God loved people so much that he had made a plan to win them back to him. That plan was to send his own Son, Jesus Christ, to save people from their sins.

God chose the Jewish nation to be holy and good so that Jesus could be born through them. Then John was reminded of God's special

Science, Technology & Growth

- A.D. 100. The disease of pneumonia was first identified. No cure was found until about A.D. 1940.
- A.D. 100. The disease of diabetes was first identified. No treatment was found until insulin was discovered in A.D. 1922.

Daily Life

A.D. 100. England. The Romans built the first London Bridge across the Thames River.

Jesus is the One who says that these things are true. Now he says, "Yes, I am coming soon."

Amen. Come, Lord Jesus!

Revelation 22:20

The Dead Sea Scrolls

When this message reached the edge of the Dead Sea, the religious Jews living there left. They took a little food and other things only. But before they left, they hid their Scripture scrolls in some large pottery jars and put them in nearby caves. They hoped the Romans would not find them there, and they could come back later and get them.

The Jews were never able to come back for their precious scrolls. And the Romans did not find them. So they lay hidden in those caves for almost 2,000 years.

In the winter of 1946–47, three shepherds were looking after their goats in that same area. The Dead Sea was in front of them, and the caves were behind them. One of the shepherds saw a small hole in the cliff. He threw a stone into the hole and heard a clinking noise. The youngest of the shepherds crawled through a larger hole next to the first one. He dropped into a small cave and saw what the stone had hit. An old pot was lying on the floor. It was broken. More pots were lying around, too.

law for the Jews given to Moses. And he saw how God had taken care of his people all through the ages by sending them judges, kings, and prophets to bring them back to him.

Finally, John saw Jesus Christ himself, and he was dazzling! Jesus was fighting Satan's armies. And Jesus won the war! Satan was defeated, and Christians were brought to live with

DID YOU KNOW THAT...

The word "revelation" means to "take the lid off" of something so you can look inside? God took the lid off his eternal plan to save us and let John look inside. Then John told us what he saw— victory!

What they had found were the Scripture scrolls of the Jews. They sold them for $93. These scrolls turned out to be some of the most important scrolls ever found in Palestine. They are called the Dead Sea Scrolls. And today, they are worth millions of dollars. But they are worth so much more to us as Christians because they show that Jesus was real!

Jesus and God forever. Christians would have the final victory over evil.

The Truth

The dream that John saw is true. And someday, when Jesus comes back again, Christians will be taken to live in that wonderful city called heaven forever and ever. God has not forgotten his promise to save his people. We will have the final victory over Satan and evil. So we must pray, "Come soon, Lord Jesus!"

BIBLE MYSTERY What did John see falling down out of heaven in his dream?

Answer: He saw hailstones that weighed over one hundred pounds each! How would you like to get hit by one of those? See Revelation 16:21.

Revelation
To John

From Then

...Till Now

A.D. 93

A.D. 96

A.D. 2,000

A.D. 79—Mt. Vesuvius erupts, bury-
ing the Roman city of Pompeii.
A.D. 80—The building of the
Colosseum is completed in Rome.

A.D. 306—Constantine becomes
emperor of the West.
A.D. 316—Emperor Constantine is
converted to Christianity.

A.D. 1776—The
Declaration of
Independence
is signed in
America.

A.D. 96–Now

God Still Loves Us

History & Politics

- A.D. 433. Attila the Hun began to reign.
- A.D. 981. Greenland. Eric the Red settled in Greenland.
- A.D. 1000. North America. The Vikings explored this region.
- A.D. 1190. Asia. Genghis Khan began his conquest of Asia.
- A.D. 1337–1437. England, France. The Hundred Years' War was fought.
- A.D. 1620. North America. The Pilgrims from England founded the Plymouth Colony.

*A*lmost two thousand years have passed since John saw the revelation from heaven and the Bible was finished. That's about the same amount of time from the time of Abraham to when Jesus was born. During that time many exciting things have happened in the world. People have lived and died. Rulers have reigned and fallen. Countries have come and gone. Inventions have been built, and older inventions have stopped being used.

In the last two thousand years, the world has changed a lot. We have come from riding donkeys to driving cars, riding on trains, flying in airplanes, and even traveling in spaceships to the moon and back. We have come from writing on animal skins, to typewriters, to computers, to sending messages all over the world on the internet. We have moved from simple outdoor amphitheaters to silent movies, "talkies," Technicolor, three-dimensional films, wrap-around sound, and now to virtual reality computer programs.

God Is Still There

Through all of these amazing changes, God has still been with us. When we are having hard times, God is with us, helping us get through them. He hears us when we pray to him, just as he heard Jesus and Paul and the apostles.

God is still in control of the world. He sets up governments, puts rulers in office, and guides the people who are at war. He is still taking care of the church, his special people in the world. He gives us courage and hope to go on. And he tells us through the Bible that we will be with him forever in heaven someday.

Our Job

Some things in the world have not changed. As Christians, we still have a special job to do, just as the Jews had a special job to do. Jesus told his apostles before he went back to heaven that he wanted his followers to tell people everywhere in the world the Good News about

- A.D. 1914–1918. World War I was in progress.
- A.D. 1933–45. Germany. Adolf Hitler and the Nazi party tried to destroy all Jewish people in the Holocaust.

- A.D. 1939–45. World War II was in progress.

Literature & Theater

- A.D. 1000–1450. Christian drama was being performed. These were called "mystery" plays. Many people could not read, so the plays helped them get to know the stories in the Bible. These plays were acted out on wagons called pageants, which they moved around the town between performances.
- A.D. 1215. England. The Magna Carta was signed by King John.
- A.D. 1279. China. Kublai Khan founded the Yuan Dynasty.
- A.D. 1599. England. The famous Globe Theater opened in London.
- A.D. 1564–1616. England. Shakespeare lived. He wrote thirty-six plays, both tragedies and comedies.

- A.D. 1611. England. The King James Version of the Bible was completed.
- A.D. 1859. Charles Darwin published his Origin of the Species. This work states Darwin's false theory of how people evolved from animals.

Religion, Philosophy & Learning

- A.D. 115. Syria, North Mesopotamia. Christianity spread quickly through these areas.
- A.D. 570–632. Middle East. Muhammad lived. His teachings, called the Koran, formed the basis of the false religion of Islam.
- A.D. 936. India. The religion of Zoroaster arrived in India.
- A.D. 1224–74. Italy. Thomas Aquinas, Italian philosopher and Roman Catholic Church theologian lived.
- A.D. 1431. Jeanne d' Arc, a leader of the French forces, was accused of being a witch by the English. She was falsely tried and convicted. Then she was burned at the stake.
- A.D. 1487. Spain. The Spanish Inquisition was begun by Ferdinand and Isabella.
- A.D. 1483–1546. Germany. A Roman Catholic priest named Martin Luther led

DID YOU KNOW THAT...

Jesus' church is a place for sinners? That's right! It's because we are sinners that Jesus died and built his church so we can be saved. The church is like a hospital; it's a place for people to come and get well spiritually.

him. As his followers today we are now his prophets and teachers in the world. He has sent us to bring people back to him. We must tell our friends, our families, and our neighbors that God loves them, that God wants them to be his children, and that God wants them to live with him in heaven.

Just as Jesus died to save the Jews and the non-Jews of his time, he died to save us, too. As the Bible says in John 3:16, "God loved the world (us!) so much that he gave his only Son… so that whoever believes in him (us!) may not be lost, but have eternal life." Thank you, God, for your amazing gift of love, grace, and salvation.

the Protestant Reformation against the Catholic Church.

- A.D. 1509–64. France. John Calvin, leader of the Protestant Reformation in France, lived.
- A.D. 1624–91. England. George Fox, founder of the protestant Society of Friends (also known as the Quakers) lived.
- A.D. 1700s. The Age of Enlightenment.
- A.D. 1703–91. England. John Wesley lived and founded the Methodist Church.

Visual Arts

- A.D. 118. Rome. The great Forum was begun. It was the world's largest concrete dome, supported by walls twenty feet thick.
- A.D. 1300–1500. The world's greatest artistic masters were working: Michelangelo, Leonardo da Vinci, Botticelli, Raphael, and Rembrandt. Many of the paintings of these great masters are on display in important museums around the world still today.

Music

- A.D. 284. Rome. Music was used at big public events, such as the athletic games in the Roman Colosseum. A huge concert was once held at the games. There were 100 trumpets, 100 horns, and 200 pipes. The Christians believed these events were evil and linked instrumental music with false religions.
- A.D. 300. Rome. A Roman bishop named Ambrose collected chants to be used in the

Roman Catholic Church. These are known as the Ambrosian Chants.

- A.D. 300–400. Rome. Christianity became a legal religion in the Roman Empire. The empire divided in A.D. 410 into eastern and western. Then two different kinds of music also began. The music of the western empire in Rome became the basis of western classical music.
- A.D. 900. Music in two or more parts began to be performed. A second, third, or fourth melody was sung above or below the plainsong or chant.
- A.D. 1473. The first complete piece of music was printed; before this each piece had to be hand copied. Printing increased the demand for music by the general public. So more and more music was written.
- A.D. 1644–1737. Italy. Antonio Stradivari, known as Stradivarius, lived and made the most famous violins in the world.
- A.D. 1709. Italy. The piano was invented by Bartolomeo Cristofori.
- A.D. 1685–1759. Germany. George Frederick Handel lived and wrote such amazing works as *Messiah*, which many choirs still sing today.
- A.D. 1685–1750. Germany. Johann Sebastian Bach lived and composed.

- A.D. 1756–91. Germany. One of the most famous composers of all time, Mozart, lived and wrote. Mozart was a musical genius, even as a child. Much of his music is still enjoyed today.

- A.D. 1770–1827. Germany. Ludwig van Beethoven, a student of Mozart, lived and composed.

NOTE: Many other great composers and musicians, too many to name, have lived and composed during these wonderful years.

Science, Technology & Growth

- A.D. 200. A medical scientist named Galen discovered how blood moves through the human body.

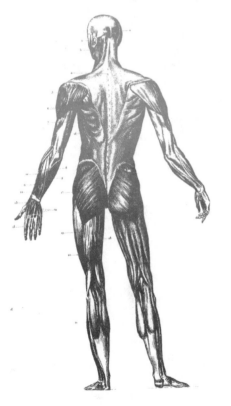

- A.D. 200–300. China. The wheelbarrow was developed.
- A.D. 600. Italy. Pretzels were invented by an Italian monk (religious man). They were given as a reward to children who learned their prayers.
- A.D. 900. The deadly disease of smallpox was first identified. A vaccine was discovered by Edward Jenner in A.D. 1796.
- A.D. 900. The disease of measles was first identified. A vaccine was not discovered until A.D. 1963.
- A.D. 1286. Italy. The first eyeglasses were made in Pisa.
- A.D. 1454. The movable-type printing press was invented.
- A.D. 1490. China. The toothbrush was invented.
- A.D. 1643. The deadly disease, typhoid fever, was first identified. A vaccine was finally found about A.D. 1888.
- A.D. 1675. Scarlet fever was first identified. Its cure, penicillin, was found in the A.D. 1940s.
- A.D. 1750–1850. The Industrial Revolution. This was the time when people began using machines to do a lot of their work for them. Many steam-powered machines and electrical machines were invented and used.
- A.D. 1873. North America. The typewriter was invented by Christopher Latham Sholes.
- A.D. 1876. North America. The telephone was invented by Alexander Graham Bell.
- A.D. 1903. North America. The airplane was invented by Wilbur and Orville Wright.
- A.D. 1906. The first animated cartoon was made.

- A.D. 1928. The first color television was invented.
- A.D. 1961. U.S.S.R. The first manned space-flight.
- A.D. 1969. North America. The United States landed the first man on the moon.
- A.D. 1972. North America. Video games were invented.

NOTE: Many other kinds of inventions were developed during these years. There are far too many to name.

Daily Life

- A.D. 700. South America. Tomatoes were being grown for food.
- A.D. 1200. Germany. Birthday cakes were first used to celebrate children's birthdays. Candles on the cake were kept lit all day to stand for life.
- A.D. 1351. Russia. The deadly disease called the Bubonic Plague reached Russia. Over 75 million people died from the plague in Europe.
- A.D. 1520. Spain. Chocolate was first brought to Spain by Aernan Cortes.
- A.D. 1600. Holland. Doughnuts were first made, but they did not have a hole in them until about A.D. 1850!
- A.D. 1666. England. First cheddar cheese was made in a small English village named (what else?) "Cheddar."
- A.D. 1886. North America. Coca-Cola™ and Dr. Pepper™ were first made and sold.
- A.D. 1900. North America. The first hamburger was made in New Haven, Connecticut, by a restaurant owner. Hot dogs were also first made that year.
- A.D. 1948. North America. The first McDonald's restaurant opened in California.

NOTE: Many other exciting developments took place during these years.

How We Got the Bible

God's Word, the Bible, has been very carefully saved for us today. The Bible was written by God. He inspired ("breathed") his thoughts into the minds of the forty men who wrote them down for people to read.

Care in copying. When ancient copies were made of God's Word, they were copied by men called scribes. Every time a scribe sat down to write, he would say, "I am writing the Law in the name of its holiness and the name of God in its holiness." He would read the sentence he was about to copy. Then he would read it again out loud. Finally, he would write the sentence. Each time a scribe wrote the name of God, he would say, "I am writing the name of God for the holiness of his name."

When a scribe finished copying a Bible book, he would count all the words and letters in the original book and in the one he was writing to be certain they were exactly the same. He would find the middle word and the middle letter in each one to make sure they were the same. By being very careful in this way, the scribe kept from making mistakes.

Printing. Hundreds of years later, when printing presses were invented, people began printing many copies of the Bible at one time. When the Bible was prepared for printing, editors and scholars were extremely careful not to make any mistakes in God's Word. They still are today.

The Bible is the most special book ever written. It is the story of God's love from the beginning of time until today. It teaches us how to live and how to remain friends with God. So we, too, must keep it safe for the people who will live after us.

From Then... ...Till Now

A.D. 95 — A.D. 2,000

- A.D. 105—Paper is invented in China.
- A.D. 130—The false religion of Taoism is accepted in China.
- A.D. 135—The suppression of the Jewish revolt leads to the dispersion (diaspora) of the Jews.
- A.D. 170—Persecution of Christians increases in Rome.
- A.D. 220—The Han dynasty ends in China.
- A.D. 257—The Visigoths and Ostrogoths invade the Black Sea region.
- A.D. 306—Constantine becomes emperor of the West.
- A.D. 316—Emperor Constantine is converted to Christianity.

- A.D. 600—Smallpox spreads from India to Europe.
- A.D. 632—Muhammad, the founder of the false religion, Islam, dies.
- A.D. 730—Printing begins in China.
- A.D. 800—Irish monks reach Iceland.
- A.D. 1000—Leif Eriksson, son of Eric the Red, explores the coast of North America.
- A.D. 1130—Stained glass is first used to decorate churches.
- A.D. 1163—Building of Notre Dame Cathedral is begun.
- A.D. 1204—Amsterdam is founded in Europe.
- A.D. 1215—King John signs the Magna Carta.

- A.D. 1295—Marco Polo brings a pasta recipe from Asia to Italy
- A.D. 1300—The use of eyeglasses becomes common.
- A.D. 1492—Christopher Columbus sets sail in search of a new path to India.
- A.D. 1776—The Declaration of Independence is signed in America
- A.D. 1861—Abraham Lincoln is inaugurated as the 16th president of the U.S.A.

Lists

...of Bible Stories
...of Historical Articles
...of Important Events

List of Bible Stories

(in alphabetical order)

Bible Story
Page

List of Historical Articles
(in alphabetical order by title)

List of Important Bible Times Events
(in historical order
by approximate date)

Date	Event
B.C.	
Beginning of Time	God Made the World and People
3000–2500	Noah and the Great Flood
2400	Languages Confused at Babel
2091	Abraham's Promise from God
2066	Isaac Was Born
2006	Twin Nations Were Born
1885	Joseph Sold into Slavery in Egypt
1876	Israel Moved to Egypt
1526	Baby Moses
1446	God Rescued Israel from Egypt
1445–1406	God Gave Israel the Ten Commandments and the Law of Moses
1406–1400	Joshua Led Israel to Conquer the Promised Land
1400–1380	God Sent Judges To Israel
1100	Ruth and Boaz
1090	Samson: God's Strongest Man
1043	Saul: Israel's First King
1004	David: Israel's Second King
971–960	Solomon: Israel's Third King and the Temple Was Built
931	Kingdom of Israel Divided
870	Elijah the Prophet
852	Elisha the Prophet
845	Obadiah the Prophet
825	Joel the Prophet

Date	Event
775	Jonah and the Big Fish
770	Hosea the Prophet
765	Amos the Prophet
740	Isaiah the Prophet
735	Micah the Prophet
723–721	Assyria Captured Israel
701	Sennacherib Attacked Judah
650	Nahum the Prophet
635	Zephaniah the Prophet
626	Jeremiah the Prophet
621	The Book of God's Law Was Found
610	Habakkuk the Prophet
601	Daniel Interpreted Nebuchadnezzar's Dream
597	Israel Taken As Slaves to Babylon
592	Ezekiel the Prophet
588–586	Jerusalem Captured by Babylon
584	The Fiery Furnace
572	Ezekiel's Dream about the Temple
562	Nebuchadnezzar Believed in God
542	God's Finger Wrote on the Wall
541	Daniel Saved from Lions by God
538	Israel Returned to Jerusalem
520	Haggai and Zechariah the Prophets
516	The New Temple Was Finished
480	Esther Saved the Jews
465	Malachi the Prophet
444–25	Walls of Jerusalem Rebuilt and Dedicated
323	Ptolomies Came to Power
201	Rome Overcame Hannibal
163–143	Maccabean War
63	Pompey Attacked Palestine
37	Herod Became King of Judea

Date	Event
27	Augustus Caesar Brought Peace to Rome
6–4	Jesus' Birth Was Told
3	Jesus Was Born and Shepherds Came to See Him
2–1	Wise Men Traveled to See Jesus
1	Joseph, Mary, and Jesus Escaped into Egypt

A.D.

Date	Event
0–27	Jesus' Childhood and Young Adulthood
27	John the Baptist and Jesus Began Their Ministries
27–30	Miracles and Teachings of Jesus
30	Jesus Died, Was Buried, Came Back to Life, Appeared to Many People, Then Went Back to Heaven
30	Holy Spirit Came on Pentecost and the Church Was Begun
32–37	Stephen Was Stoned to Death and Saul (Paul) Became a Christian
45–47	Paul's First Missionary Journey
48–50	Meeting in Jerusalem
50–95	Letters to Christians
50–51	Paul's Second Missionary Journey
53	Paul's Third Missionary Journey
58	Paul Was Put into Prison
58–60	Paul's Trials and Trip to Rome
61–63	Paul in Prison at Home
64–67	Paul in Prison for the Last Time
95	Jesus' Revelation to John